SPELLING DEAREST

The Down and Dirty, Nitty-Gritty History of English Spelling

by

Niall McLeod Waldman

Published by *What The Dickens Press*

First published by What The Dickens Press and AuthorHouse 06/16/04

ISBN: 1-4184-5906-2 (e-book)
ISBN: 1-4184-5330-7 (Paperback)

Library of Congress Control Number: 2003092592

This book is printed on acid free paper.

Printed in the United States of America
Bloomington, IN

For additional information on the subject of English spelling, frequently asked questions, artwork purchasing information, and promotional giveaways visit www.spellingdearest.com

To order additional copies of *Spelling Dearest*
visit www.Authorhouse.com
or phone 1-888-280-7715

Comments or questions
nmwaldman@spellingdearest.com
nmwaldman@aol.com

TABLE OF CONTENTS

DEDICATION

To Mo and Ko because their names rhyme.

FOREWORD

In his book, Niall McLeod Waldman sets out to find the forces, developments, and individuals responsible for driving our spelling away from its phonetic base. He figures, if we can pinpoint where and how we went wrong, we may have a chance to fix our crippled spelling.

We have here the first of perhaps two volumes. The practical title of the second, if we ever see it, might be, *How Can We Rescue Our Spelling from Its Present Waste and Confusion?*

Dr. Abraham F. Citron, Ph.D.
Professor Emeritus, Wayne State University
Founder of BEtSS
(Better Education thru Simplified Spelling)

ACKNOWLEDGMENT

I wish first of all to express my deep appreciation to the numerous experts on various aspects of the English language who have been quoted throughout this manuscript. The mere mention of their names has brought credibility to these pages. In addition to their quotations I would like to thank them for the mountain of enlightening facts which I obtained from their conversations, correspondence, and from studying their published writings.

For editorial advice, suggestions, and encouragement thanks to the following people: Jonathan Bocknek, Joyce Hampton, Gail Corbett, Nora Robson, Dorrie O'Brien, and Abe Citron.

Most importantly, though, I would like to convey my gratitude to all the individuals who ridiculed my less-than-perfect spelling through the years. Their constant badgering motivated and fueled me to write this. Thanks to one and all.

GLOSSARY

English Spelling: Spelling that evolved in the United Kingdom and is used with various minor modifications by English-speaking people around the world.

British Spelling: The spelling used by the people of the United Kingdom.

American Spelling: The spelling used by the people of the United States of America.

Spelling (in general): Simple letters grouped together to express subtle thoughts in the most complicated configuration possible.

INTRODUCTION

According to the written testimony of a great many knowledgeable experts, the English language has by far "the worst and most irrational and inconsistent alphabetic spelling system in the entire world."[1] Not the worst in the continent, and not the worst in the northern hemisphere, nor simply the worst in the West, but the worst in the whole God-forsaken world. So our spelling system isn't just bad, it's worse than anybody could ever imagine — it's worse than the worst there is. There's heavy-duty bad and there's industrial-strength bad. Well, this system is big-bang bad. To think, all this time I, and millions like me, were convinced it was *our* fault we can't spell. How wrong we were.

In 1982, Dr. Stanley L. Sharp, author of *The REAL Reason Why Johnny Still Can't Read*, stated "there are at least 50 million adults in the United States who do not spell well." Unfortunately, nothing has improved since he wrote this. As a matter of fact, with the population explosion and our increased reliance on computers to correct our spelling, the situation has most definitely taken a turn for the worse.[2] In his text, Dr. Sharp calls people who have trouble spelling, "poor spellers." Not "occasionally wrong spellers" or "bad spellers of hard words", but "poor spellers." Now I'm not sure what his definition of a poor speller is, but mine is that it's someone who isn't rich enough to be able to afford a secretary, but it's someone who needs one badly. And to think there are at least 50 million of them on the loose in the U.S. That translates, taking into account the age of the estimate, to approximately a third of the adult population. This means one out of every three Americans who are old enough to survive on their own, can't. They need ghostwriters to write their Christmas cards for them.

How on earth in an advanced and civilized country like the U.S. can there be this many people who can't spell? It can't be blamed on poor memory, because many people with terrific memories can remember just about everything — except spelling.[3] Oh, they forget the usual things like whether a stalactite comes from the top or bottom of a cave, for instance, but that's normal; everyone forgets that. So, who or what is to blame for this poor spelling situation? Good spellers blame bad spellers for their own incompetence. Bad spellers blame their genes. The previous owners of these genes stomp up to school (in two halves) and blame the teachers. In the end, a growing number of teachers blame the spelling *system* for our problems because there's no one else to point to.

I believe these teachers are right. The *system* is to blame. Our illogical, inconsistent, and unreliable method for combining letters to form words is the primary — and sometimes the only — reason for people's inability to spell. Only teachers — who understand the system as much as anybody can, yet are faced with teaching children who understand the system as much as anybody can't — realize it. These teachers still deduct for errors, but in their hearts they know that it's our stupid spelling system that's at fault, not the supposedly brain-damaged children who can't learn it.

Contrary to what some might think, not all countries of the world have multitudes of children with serious spelling problems. For instance, children from countries with phonetic spelling systems (i.e., systems with words spelled the way they sound) have very little difficulty learning to spell. As a matter of fact, in countries such as Italy, Germany, Spain, and Finland, children rarely even use spelling books at school because their systems are so easy to learn.[4] What confidence these youngsters must have, knowing they are masters of their own language, and what a bond they must have with their own country, when at any given moment they are patriotic enough to be able to spell its name.

Here, in direct contrast, are a few of the endless list of things that make spelling difficult for *our* children. We have too many silent consonants such as the *l* in *walk* and the *t* in *mortgage*; we have too many illogical vowel combinations such as the *ai* in *said* and the *eau* in *bureau*; we have too many double letters such as the double *p* in *sapphire* and the double *u* in *vacuum*; we have too many words that sound the same but are spelled differently, such as *rain, rein,* and *reign*; and we have more than our share of words that sound different but are spelled the same, such as *tear* (eye fluid) and *tear* (to rip apart). Additionally, we have an overabundance of nuisance spellings such as *colonel, queue,* and *choir,* which have no redeeming qualities whatsoever.

On top of that, we have a gross excess of differing spellings for each of the sounds we have. The *sh* sound, for instance, has 19 spellings, including *ss* in *issue, sc* in *crescendo, ch* in *chute, ce* in *ocean,* and a single *t* in *negotiate*. There are 42 different sounds in our language and we, in our inexhaustible capacity for innovation, have invented over 400 ways to spell them.[5] That's an average of 10 spellings for every sound. No wonder millions of schoolchildren throughout the English-speaking world are confused on a daily basis. We have far too many rules and far too many exceptions to these rules, and too many people saying, "all you have to do to be able to spell is learn the rules." That's way too many things wrong with any subject.

If our complex spelling system only affected people's ability to spell, that would be bad enough. Unfortunately, though, our spelling system also plays a considerable role in the high number of adult functional illiterates in the United States and other English-speaking countries. In all the major English-speaking countries, 17 to 24 percent of the adult population is functionally illiterate, whereas in countries with more phonetic spelling systems, such as Finland and Germany, the figures are about half that amount. Furthermore, nothing we've ever done to improve our teaching methods ever closes that gap significantly, because we're fighting an uphill battle with downhill skis. We don't have the correct equipment for the task: an easily understandable spelling system.

All right, so our complex spelling system is greatly to blame for our poor spelling and reading abilities — but who or what is to blame for the complex spelling system, and how did it become as bad as it is? The answer to these and many other important questions can be found, along with an Anglo-Saxon recipe for barbecued missionary, in the history that's about to unfold.

THE

HISTORY

OF

ENGLISH SPELLING

Old English

Chapter 1
THE SIMPLE START OF
OLD ENGLISH

Let's clarify one thing before we get started. The Old-English language wasn't called *old* back in the Old-English days, mainly because it wasn't old to the people who lived then. Indeed, with the wars that were being waged, coupled with the improvements to crossbows and catapults, what reason had these people to believe their language would live long enough to become Middle- or Modern English anyway?

To add to the confusion, not only was the Old-English language not called *old* back in the Old-English days, it wasn't even called *English*. Instead, among other things, it was referred to as *Englisc*. This sounds to me like German — which as you will soon find out is *almost* exactly what it was.

The English language began in the middle of the fifth century when the Germanic-speaking tribes, the Angles and Saxons and Jutes, invaded the Celtic-speaking people who lived at the time in what is now called England. When I say *invaded*, what I really mean is *slaughtered*, because by all accounts these Germanic-speaking tribes seem to have massacred the poor Celtic people. Bede, the famous eighth-century English historian, summed the situation up most succinctly in his best-selling publication, *A History of the English Church and People*, when he wrote: "priests were slain at the altar; bishops and people alike, regardless of rank, were destroyed with fire and

3

sword, and none remained to bury those who had suffered a cruel death."[6] This shows just how frightening these invaders must have been because if *none* remained to bury the dead, it means that all the Celts who weren't slaughtered on the spot ran off as fast as their little terror-stricken Celtic legs could carry them.

Bede's account is probably an exaggeration (given that it was written by a man of the church about invading heathens). Nevertheless, there seems to be little doubt that a large portion of the Celts who survived the Anglo-Saxon invasion did so only by escaping onto or over the Cambrian mountains into what is now called Wales. Why the invading Germanic tribes (also known as the Anglo-Saxons or Saxons) didn't follow the Celts and finish them off isn't completely clear. I'd be willing to wager, however, it had something to do with the mountains. I bet, as soon as the Celts climbed onto the Cambrians and became Welsh, they started to sing, and that singing caused their perfectly-tuned voices to echo through the valleys, making it sound like there were millions of them. Consequently, the Saxons decided to let them off with a warning this time. Unfortunately for the Saxons, the Celts weren't so forgiving; they raided and battled the Saxons along the Welsh border for centuries.

Some of the Celts also escaped across the channel to Brittany or fled over rough terrain to Cornwall and southwestern Scotland. These settlements, along with Wales, are now collectively called *The Celtic Fringe,* much to the annoyance of the Celts who much prefer the term *Lunatic Fringe* because of its greater tendency to deter further Anglo-Saxon advancement.

Why the Saxons were never able to take over what is now called Scotland is another point that isn't fully clear. I suspect, however, it had a lot to do with the following. The ancient Scottish were a tough bunch of caber-tossers who even the Romans couldn't conquer. They demonstrated that toughness by walking about in the freezing cold highland weather with no

4

pants or underwear on, just a piece of tartan wrapped round their middle. Obviously the Anglo-Saxons took one look at them and concluded that a people as crazy as this weren't about to be talked into submission. So after a succession of customary borderline skirmishes and the occasional token infiltration and settlement, the Anglo-Saxons let them off with a warning, too.

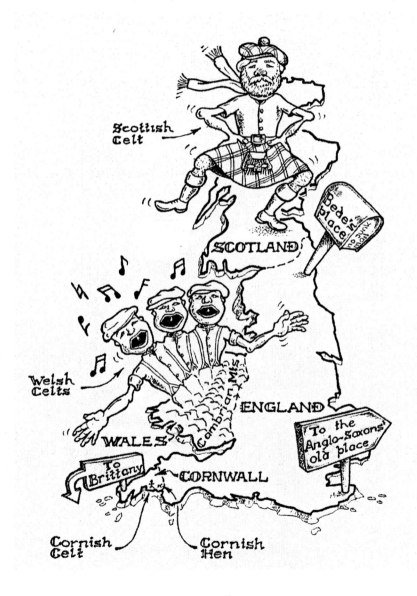

Long before the battles along the Celtic Fringe were over, the English language (which in those days was a mixture of Germanic dialects) was free to spread itself across most of England.[7] Once it did this, the years that followed proved to have the simplest form of spelling our language has ever known. In fact, I would go so far as to say that those years produced the simplest form of spelling any language has ever known, because there *was* no English spelling back then. How could there be — there was no English *writing*! (There was an ancient Germanic magical-marking system called Runic, which was engraved on weapons and other valuable items, but that didn't develop into the English-writing system we have today.)[8]

This uncomplicated English-spelling-free utopia was short-lived, though. Its protective bubble burst at the end of the sixth century when the very first words were written in what would eventually grow to be the English-writing system of today. As far as spelling is concerned, it's been downhill all the way ever since — apart from the occasional leveling off or free-fall to break the monotony.

We're in a leveling-off period now, but that, I suspect, is only because we've hit rock-bottom already. And judging from the mess we're in, it was after one of those free falls. What's more, the landing was so severe that spelling is now being kept alive by machines, namely word processors, electronic dictionaries, and perhaps the most machine-like of all, good spellers.

INVADER'S TRIBE   Three tribes invaded Britain at this time: the Angles, the Saxons, and the Jutes. The Angles & the Saxons are immortalized in the name Anglo-Saxon. The Jutes, on the other hand, are a bit like Pete Best & Stuart Sutcliffe of the Beatles; they were there at the beginning, but very few people remember them.

ANCIENT-GERMANIC MAGICAL MARKINGS (POSSIBLE TRANSLATION) "If you can read this you're too close — hasta la vista baby."

ANGLO-SAXON INVADER

Chapter 2
THE COMPLICATED MIDDLE OF OLD ENGLISH

English writing, and therefore English spelling, started about 1400 years ago when a Roman Catholic monk, later to be known as St. Augustine, refounded the Christian church in southern England.[9] This, in my eyes, makes St. Augustine one of the bad guys, because if he hadn't done what he did then, we might not have what we have now — the worst alphabetic spelling system in the world.

St. Augustine, along with 40 of his Benedictine brethren, arrived on English soil in the spring of 597. He was sent by Pope Gregory I to convert the heathen English. This he did, and with such efficiency that by Christmas Day that same year he was baptizing thousands. Christening so many individuals after such a short while is truly an astonishing feat. It is, however, even more astonishing than it first seems, because the Anglo-Saxon people back then were renowned for their viciousness and savagery. They did everything imaginable to the people who annoyed them (I'm not even sure cannibalism was out of the question) and there was St. Augustine half-drowning them in water and they didn't do a thing to retaliate!

Christians will undoubtedly conclude that the Anglo-Saxons' passivity and the smoothness of their conversion was the unmistakable work of the Almighty, but I believe there was a much more powerful force at work: blind luck. It was blind luck, for instance, that led St. Augustine, when he first arrived on English soil, to land in an area where there already was a small Christian community. And it was blind luck — with four-leaf clovers and rabbits' feet you can rub — that the wife of the king of that territory was already Christian.

Not everyone who knows about this period in history would attach as much importance to this blind-luck factor as I do. Nevertheless, I would go so far as to say that if these fortunate circumstances hadn't occurred, St. Augustine and his merry band of missionaries would only be remembered in encyclopedias for having *tasted just like chicken.*

Having said that, I'm also of the opinion that the English population's reading habits, after St. Augustine arrived, played an important part in the spreading of Christianity. Not many people could read then, but they could be read to. And since a great deal of what was read to them was religious, many of them became Christians without even realizing it. They just woke one morning and that was it, they were Christians — no more killing people just for fun and no more sleeping in until noon on Sundays.

It was hard to avoid reading about religion in those days. Even ancient Anglo-Saxon legends had religious themes written into them after the arrival of St. Augustine.[10] So not only were the people converted to Christianity, their history was, too.

During this reading and writing and conversion process, people came face to face with English spelling for the first time — and little did they know how much trouble that chance encounter would eventually bring them. Don't get me wrong, though. I'm not saying St. Augustine personally did things to our spelling that made it become as bad as it is. Any inclination toward that assumption would be pure speculation on my part, especially since no record of St. Augustine's English writing has survived. What's more, I'm not even sure St. Augustine actually wrote anything in English. Maybe he just dictated to one of his followers, "Take a letter, Brother Dominic. Dear Pope Greg: About the English muffins you requested. They don't have any. Kindest regards, Augustine."

Once again, however, for me to assume that one of St. Augustine's followers did all his writing for him would also be pure speculation. St. Augustine died around 604 AD, and no record of *any* English writing has survived from before that time.[11] This means no one really knows who wrote what or how it was written. Or, more importantly, what kind of muffins the Pontiff requested. All I know for sure is that St. Augustine was there at the beginning when English spelling started. Therefore, all I'm blaming him for is authorizing the start of what eventually became the most blackboard-scratching part of our language.

Spelling is annoying. Millions of unsatisfied customers can attest to that. It's annoying like an itch inside a cast when there isn't a coat hanger in sight, or like a mosquito up your nostril at any time. For all I know, though, St. Augustine may very well have started it off completely irritant-free by making it phonetic. In fact, why would he do otherwise? When St. Augustine arrived on English soil, nobody could read or write a word of English. Nobody in the entire world, that is, not even the English. Wouldn't you make your spelling phonetic in a situation like that?

Regrettably, though, St. Augustine not only couldn't read or write English when he arrived, he couldn't speak it, either. So I wonder whose speech-pattern his spelling was based on — his or the natives'? If it was his, there's the slight problem of accent to consider. St. Augustine's accent must have been stronger than the blind luck that accompanied it.

Still, as I said, I'm not blaming St. Augustine for everything. After all, he only lingered seven years in his new country before Pope God the First decided in his infinite wisdom that the rental time on his skin-suit had ended. How much damage can someone do in that time? You be the judge. All I'm certain is that somewhere between St. Augustine's arrival and the start of the 10th century, when there are enough records for historians to come to educated conclusions, spelling had already become quite annoying — mostly because the historians can't agree on whether it was phonetic or not. *My* assessment of the situation, based on the evidence they've presented, is that it was a little of each: a little phonetic, a little unphonetic, *and* a little annoying.

ST. AUGUSTINE

As unfavorable as my assessment already is, I haven't yet given the total picture of the horrible state of English spelling in this period. For starters, I haven't mentioned that there were four main dialects in England at this time, each with its own region and each with its own system of spelling.[12] This means that in the country as a whole, there could be a number of different, perfectly legitimate phonetic spellings all for the same word. That kind of thing could give phonetic spelling a bad name — and probably did.

Something else I haven't mentioned yet is that each dialect region had also developed by this time its very own traditional spellings. Traditional spellings are spellings that probably used to be phonetic, but through the years their pronunciation changed while the tradition of how they were spelled didn't. That kind of thing is even worse than the phonetic spelling mix-up. It could give the whole of our spelling system a bad name — and definitely has.

Nothing acts alone, all the same. It's the combination of phonetic and traditional spellings, plus the dialect regions, plus a bunch of other irregularities that has led me to conclude that, overall, the spelling in England during this period was a practical demonstration of the definition of the word *yuck!* Sadly, there wasn't the political will or the public want back then to make things better.

A SMALL SAMPLE OF THE MANY VARIED SPELLINGS FROM THE COMPLICATED MIDDLE OF OLD ENGLISH	
MODERN-DAY SPELLING	VARIATIONS FROM THE MIDDLE OF OLD ENGLISH
heaven	heofon, heofen, heofne
earth	eorðe, eorðo, eorþan
today	to deg, todaez, todaege
forgive	forgif, forzef, forgeaf
evil	yfle, yfel, yfele

Some of the above Old-English letters are obsolete in Modern English. Here are their names and Modern-English equivalents:
þ (thon) = th; ð (eth) = th; ʒ (yogh) = g.

After all that's been said, there is one thing about this period that has made it less undesirable than it otherwise might have been. Our present-day worst enemies, silent consonants, were for the most part unheard of back then.[13] Of course, silent consonants are always unheard of, hence the name, but theirs were also unseen. Now there's a combination — silent and invisible; we could make use of letters like that today. I bet if we did, though, the self-appointed protectors of all that's complex would insist we keep the spaces.

Armies of experts offer all sorts of plausible explanations for spelling becoming what it became in the middle of the Old-English period. I, however, being a little less guarded than these experts (and not subject to the same reasonable constraints of logic as they are) think that the monks who came after St. Augustine are to blame. Specifically, the monks in the scriptoriums (writing houses) whose lifetime employment and enjoyment was to copy manuscripts that were composed by other people.

My unsubstantiated contention is that these monastic scribes deliberately allowed spelling to become worse than it once was because they wanted spelling to be as difficult as it possibly could be. The purpose of this seemingly wacko behavior was quite sensible, really — *for monks*. They were bored out their skulls and they figured a little unnecessary complication would make their otherwise mundane existences more exciting.

Disbelievers will say, "if these monks were that bored, why couldn't they have found other ways to stimulate themselves without messing with our spelling system?" How could they find other ways to stimulate themselves, though? They didn't do anything else. They just scribed all day, then went to bed. And they never did anything in bed that was exciting — writer's cramp after a long day at the scriptorium saw to that.

Not until the next period, when a real live king asserted his regal influence, did the monks relent a little. This allowed spelling to become slightly better. Who says royalty don't earn their keep? That's one good deed in the 500 years since the English language started. Give them a break!

Chapter 3
THE STABILIZING END OF OLD ENGLISH

From the fragmentation and diversity of the last period, there emerged at the end of the 10th century, a nationwide spelling system that was almost as stable as our own. Almost as stable as our own, but nowhere near as complex yet — although still complex nonetheless. Not all examples of late Old-English writing that have survived to the present day used this spelling system; however, the bulk of them did.[14]

The *Lord's Prayer* (dated about 1000 AD)[15]
(Typical Late Old-English stabilizing spelling)

þu ure faeder.

þe eart on heofonum.

Sy þin nama ʒehalʒod.

Cume ðin rice.

Sy ðin wylla on eorðan. swaswa on heofonum.

Syle us todaeʒ urne daʒhwamlican hlaf.

And forʒyf us ure ʒyltas

swaswa we forʒyfað ðamþe wið us aʒyltað.

And ne laed ðu na us on costnunʒe.

Ac alys us fram yfele.

Many of the letter combinations and other writing features that we recognize as English were not yet in existence in the late Old-English period. Furthermore, the Old-English alphabet had a number of different letters, including þ (thorn), ð (eth), and ȝ (yogh), which have not made it through to modern times. These factors, along with a distinct difference in vocabulary and sentence structure, make late Old-English writing resemble a foreign language. Consequently, like most foreign languages, the spelling looks many times worse than it actually is.

It is thought that this complex-looking yet relatively stable spelling system came about because of the coming to power of a king named Edgar the Peaceful.[16] I'm inclined to believe this is true because organizing things, usually in a stable manner, was the kind of activity that this king enjoyed. During his reign, Edgar organized and stabilized the country, the navy, and a host of other things. The organization most important to us here, however, was in fact a reorganization — of the church. During this reorganization, monks and priests and other scribes — vital to the writing and copying process for the whole country — embarked on a path that would eventually lead to the nationwide stabilizing of their spelling. This would mean that the spelling by a scribe in one dialect region would eventually become very much like the spelling by a scribe in most other dialect regions. These Old-Englishers were a sharp bunch. It only took them five centuries to figure out there might be some benefit to this. I'm amazed the concept of satellite communications eluded them.

The fact that stabilization was occurring nationwide at this time can be easily established by learning to read Old English and comparing the spellings of the surviving late Old-English manuscripts. Or by learning to read Modern English and believing what *A History of English Spelling* says on page seven: "a remarkably rigid spelling system [was] in use throughout England."[17] On the other hand, establishing *why* stabilization was occurring at this time is a little harder to pin down. So, instead of wasting time searching for other people's highly personal and often hypothetical explanations for this, I've devised two outrageously speculative conspiracy theories of my own.

Theory One: When Edgar gained the throne of England, the monastic scribes realized it was only a matter of time before this pathological organizer focused his organizational skills on their horrible spelling system. So rather than letting the spelling that they worked like demons to destroy take a nasty turn to the sensible, they slowly started to stabilize it. This kept spelling nice and hard, but not so obviously disorganized that King Edgar would keep it high on his daily *to-do* list.

Theory Two: The Christian world was heading toward the end of its first millennium and the monks, being God-fearing critters, were eager to get their affairs in order just in case judgment day was coming. One of the things they thought they might have to answer for was their spelling. (If *I* noticed it was much more complicated than it needed to be, I'm sure God would.) Thus, the monks had no choice but to tidy up their system just enough to avoid deity-detection and all the punishment and pestilence that goes with it.

Based on this theory, I'm amazed that we in the modern world didn't panic and do some major reconstruction to our spelling system at the end of the second millennium. After all, as the rest of this history will show, we added 1000 years of ever-increasing complexity to the system that I'm absolutely positive hasn't escaped the Big Guy's notice.

KING EDGAR'S TO-DO LIST
I. Prioritize important matters of state.
II. Alphabetize major historical events of the realm.
III. Map royal genealogy (exclude inbreeding).
IV. Stabilize English spelling (include inbreeding).

ROYAL TREATMENT
Instead of letting monks, priests, & other scribes stabilize English spelling, King Edgar should have given it the royal treatment — he should have locked it in the tower until it rotted away.

KING EDGAR

Middle English

Chapter 4
THE SIMPLE START OF
MIDDLE ENGLISH

So Edgar the Peaceful and his obsessive-compulsive alter ego, Edgar the Extremely Organized, helped us achieve, even before the Old-English period had ended, a relatively stable and comparatively useful spelling system. It was a system that was so well-established that it might still be in use today if a Norman-French duke, later named William the Conqueror, hadn't decided in the 11th century to turn England into a Norman-French province.

In 1066 this French-speaking duke and his French-speaking army, crossed over the English Channel and defeated King Harold II, the ruling English monarch of the time, at the now-famous Battle of Hastings. This battle, which eventually led to the complete Norman-French takeover of England, actually took place six and a half miles *outside* Hastings. So really, to be irritatingly precise, the Battle of Hastings should actually be called the Battle of *Near*-Hastings.

Exact names of famous battles are important, but it's the successful invasion by the French-speaking conquerors that has real significance here, because once the full effect of this linguistic infiltration was felt over the whole country, very few people wrote in English anymore. So, at least for the people who didn't write in English anymore, English spelling became as simple as it was before St. Augustine. As far as those who did write in English are concerned, who cares? If they were dumb enough to go against what everyone else in the country was doing, they deserve to be ignored. There were so few of them anyway that historians often refer to English in this period as being mainly "a spoken language."[18]

Why there was so little English writing at this time is easy to explain. The new government, new aristocracy, and new leaders of anything important were all French. Meanwhile, the old government, old aristocracy, and old leaders of anything important — in other words, all the people liable to read in English — were all dead. Either that or they were hiding out in the mountains again or pretending to be illiterate peasants who, for obvious reasons, stopped their bi-monthly delivery of the *Anglo-Saxon Chronicle* and canceled their subscription to the Old-English equivalent of *Newsweek*. Once the demand for Anglo-Saxon reading material stopped, so eventually did most of the reading material. That's one of the reasons there was very little written English in those days.[19]

The demand for *spoken* English, however, was never in danger. It not only survived the Norman invasion, it thrived because of it. It held its own as one of the two living languages in England at that time. The ruling class wrote and spoke in French and the peasants spoke and swore at them in English. Neither of the two of them bothered with English spelling.

To better understand the relationship between Normans and Saxons in this period, all a person has to do is re-read some of the legends of Robin Hood. In many of these stories, Robin, his men, and the poor are all Saxons, while the Sheriff of Nottingham and the evil Prince John are Normans. Maid Marion is a Norman in love with a Saxon, Robin the Hood.[20] In the movies, of course, everyone speaks English, but that's Hollywood.

Given the fact that the outcome of the Norman invasion was that neither the Normans nor the Saxons bothered with English spelling, perhaps it's time for a new invasion — this time an invasion of all the English-speaking countries combined — because I suspect that a takeover, like the one that took place in Britain at the Battle of *Near*-Hastings in 1066, is about the only way the English-speaking world will ever see such simple spelling again.

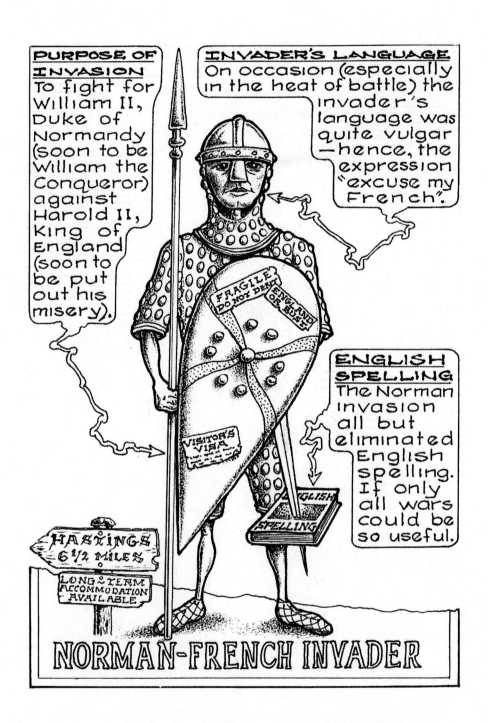

NORMAN-FRENCH INVADER

Chapter 5
THE COMPLICATED MIDDLE OF MIDDLE ENGLISH

In the mid 13th century, not long after King Philip II of France forcefully took over Normandy (the territory in France where the Normans originally came from), the Normans in England were forced to the belated realization that they were home already. As a consequence, many of them thought it was time to learn the language of their adopted country. Admittedly, a good portion of them already knew English by this time. Even so, a few individuals at the very top of that society had a great deal of trouble ordering fish and chips since they couldn't speak the language of the natives. So really, if the truth were told, the upper classes' need for greasy British fast food helped reinstate English as the spoken, as well as the written, language of England during this period.

An additional boost to the attraction toward English at this time came once again from the French. The real French, that is, from French-France, not the Norman French from Normandy. In the middle of the 13th century, these real French invaded and took over the running of England, much like the Normans had done 200 years before them. Only this time it was a peaceful invasion. They were invited in and were freely given important government positions by several English kings of the period. Once the real French settled in, however, the peacefulness started to fade because the English *and* the Normans grew to resent them. The English didn't like them much because they had very little time for the English or their language; and the Normans didn't like them because they stole the Norman's jobs and looked upon them as not much better than the English. So now the Normans not only felt at home in England, but they were being treated like they *were* English. This prompted them to decide to *be* English and, in a manner befitting their newfound nationality, they joined forces with the real English and *politely* asked the real French to leave. Then they had tea. (Tea hadn't actually arrived in England by this time, so what they really had was hot water, but they drank it out of china cups with their pinkies raised, making them well prepared for its eventual arrival.)

Although the real French left when they were politely asked, they soon returned and it took a couple of bloody battles before the united English gained the upper hand for good. Of course, through it all, the Normans constantly proved themselves worthy of being called English by always remembering to say they were sorry after they killed someone. It's British battlefield etiquette number nine. It comes right after warning enemies of surprise attacks.

It took a while, as I have shown, but once the Normans finally made up their minds that they were English, there was no holding them back. Within no time at all they were running their households and conducting their businesses in English. And that, no doubt, was the final nail in the coffin, after the fish and chips, for French as the principal language of the upper crust in England. French didn't entirely disappear during this period. It lasted quite a bit longer in legal language and royal documents. Over time, however, English reasserted itself completely.

REAL FRENCH LEGACY The Real French made the Normans realize how much they loved England. It's the universal law of patriotism: the love we have for our country is directly proportional to the hatred we have for someone else's.

OFFICIAL ROYAL INVITATION

Thou art cordially invited to peacefully take over England

The King

FREE VOUCHER The bearer of this document is entitled to one free government job. All brain cells to be removed prior to commencement.

REAL-FRENCH INVADER

The French language may have fared badly in the middle of Middle English, but French *words* were treated a lot better, because literally thousands of them found refuge in English. In fact, so many French words entered the English language at this point that I have a feeling we actually speak French and we're just too Francophobic to admit it.

A FEW OF THE MANY WORDS THAT ENTERED ENGLISH VIA THE FRENCH LANGUAGE IN THE COMPLICATED MIDDLE OF MIDDLE ENGLISH	
MODERN-DAY ENGLISH SPELLING	FRENCH SPELLING BEFORE ENTRY INTO ENGLISH
fruit	fruit
reign	reigne
sauce	sauce
beauty	beaute
heir	heir

See endnote [21]

With all the additions to the language in this period and all the disruptions to the country as a whole, no one should be astonished to discover that English spelling didn't make it through this turmoil completely unscathed. For a start, it became regionalized again — that is, different regions employed different spelling systems. These different regions, however, aren't as easy to define as the regions in the complicated bit in the middle of Old English, because on this occasion they didn't coincide with dialect boundaries. This is probably just as well because even though there were only a few major dialects in

England at this time, there were countless numbers of minor ones. In England back then every man was an island, with his own language, it seems.

This is what the book, *A History of English Spelling*, had to say about the regional spellings of this period. They were, it says, "used over a wide geographical area which incorporated more than one regional variety of spoken English."[22] This indicates that scribes must have been relying very heavily on traditional spellings again, rather than sticking to the crazy old notion that spelling should represent the actual sound of words.

Not all regions were ignoring sound, though. There was one region right at the beginning of this time span that embraced it and, as a result, developed an extremely phonetic spelling system. The area that this region covered, however, was restricted to the land mass encompassed by one pair of size-eight sandals, and it disappeared completely right after expanding to the shape of a dead monk's body. So it wasn't exactly an influential nationwide trendsetter.

One monk's phonetic spelling system may not seem important enough to mention here but it is significant in the sense of what could have been. If only that monk (known as Orm) had lived long enough to spread his system across the whole of England, our lives would be vastly improved today. Like any phonetic system, it wouldn't have been phonetic for everyone — or maybe even anyone, depending on how much of a lisp Orm had. It would, however, have been consistent, because it was, and it would have been the same system for the entire country. That at least would have been something.[23]

Regrettably, though, Orm died and any hopes of his spelling convention catching on died with him. There's no evidence of wrongdoing or foul play surrounding this monk's death; nevertheless, I'm suspicious enough to suspect murder. And we all must know what the motive was: he was a disgrace to his profession. His spelling was just too simple for his fellow monks to allow him to survive — so they took a vow and silenced him. That's one possible scenario, I'm sure there's many more.

The simplicity in the previously-mentioned spelling system, as you may have gathered, was not so much in its phonetic-ness as in its consistency. It consistently spelled the same words the same way. That was something which very few of the other regional systems of the time could be accused. Of course, as usual, these other regions had wonderful excuses for their irregularity: lack of trained scribes, scribes trained in other languages, and the collision of assorted spelling traditions come immediately to mind. The irregularity-causing factor that tops my list, however, is the abundant use of variant spellings. (A variant spelling, for the previously uninterested, is simply a well-established optional spelling. Or as the more cynical amongst us might put it, it's a wrong spelling used enough times by the right people to make it acceptable as an alternative.)

Having variant spellings at all is bad enough. In this period, however, a sizable number of these variations originated from regions other than the ones in which they were used. This doesn't seem so terrible until it is realized that manuscripts from different regions at this time often had to be translated so that people in other regions could understand them.[24] This means that at least some of the variants for some of the words in any given region must have looked like they were entirely different words.

Take these three regionally influenced variations of the word *kin* as an example: *kyn, ken, kun. Kyn* is okay, but *ken* could be a number of different Middle-English words, and *kun*. Well, let's just say if someone referred to me as a *kun* I wouldn't be thinking they were pleasantly calling me "family."[25]

To add to this chaos, the spelling in most regions, in this and the next period, took on a distinct French flavor. What this means is that an immense number of words or parts of words were spelled like the French would spell them in their language. These are the same French who didn't even sound their words the way we would sound them if they were ours. In fact, it's the same French who sometimes didn't even sound their words at all. They just shrugged their shoulders or waved their hands and that was considered to be a whole sentence. With this in mind, it should come as no surprise that many of the words or parts of words that the French gave us were riddled with silent letters. Obviously, these were the bits that were supposed to be mimed.

SOME OF THE FRENCH–INFLUENCED SPELLING CUSTOMS THAT CHANGED ENGLISH SPELLING IN THE COMPLICATED MIDDLE OF MIDDLE ENGLISH			
FRENCH-INFLUENCED CUSTOM	MODERN-DAY SPELLING OF ONE OF THE MANY AFFECTED WORDS	COMMON OLD-ENGLISH SPELLING BEFORE FRENCH INFLUENCE	MIDDLE-ENGLISH VARIANTS AFTER FRENCH INFLUENCE (SOME ARE UNINFLUENCED)
qu-spelling for kw-sound	queen	cwén	quene, quuen, qwen
c-spelling for s-sound	mice	mýs	mice, myce, myse
o-spelling for ŭ-sound	wonder	wundor	wondere, wondur, wondire
ou-spelling for oo-sound	wound (injury)	wūnd	wound, wounde, wund
h-spelling for no sound	honest	No Old-English spelling for this word	honeste, oneste, onest

See endnote [26]

29

English spelling was, to say the least, quite imperfect before the Normans arrived. Their spelling, however, plus the real French spelling, which was sometimes different, helped greatly to increase this imperfection. If pressed, I could understand the reasoning behind new English words borrowed from the French being spelled like the French would spell them. I can even accept new words created by the French in England being spelled the French way. If I was bound, gagged, and dragged behind a chariot, though, I don't think I could ever be persuaded that taking perfectly good existing English words and changing them to the French way of spelling has any worthwhile attributes at all. That, nevertheless, is exactly what happened. The word *some*, for instance, used to be spelled *sum* before the Normans arrived,[27] and the word *quick* used to be spelled *cwic* before the invasion.[28] These old spellings were phonetic for us then and are phonetic for us now, yet we changed them. I've never heard of anything so ludicrous in my life, except for maybe what happened to the word *dumb*. It was spelled *dumb* before the Norman French came and, of course, we kept it.[29] Put bluntly, it was dumb then and it's still dumb now.

Chapter 6
THE STABILIZING END OF MIDDLE ENGLISH

The first step toward this, the second stabilization period, occurred when English writing started being used again on official royal documents. This happened in the early years of the 15th century. At first, only the king's affairs were recorded in English. This I find peculiar because I would have thought that French, being the language of love, would have been much more appropriate for recording something as intimate as an affair. Still, I guess the king figured there was enough French in English and enough Latin in French (before it came into English) to make English enough of a *romance* language to handle that subject on its own.[30]

Soon the use of written English expanded beyond the king and was used by royal scribes to record the official business of the whole country. Out of that expanded use grew a *stabilizing* spelling system so enticing that before long the best scribes in the nation were all being influenced by it.

I have called this spelling system *stabilizing* because after analyzing hundreds of 15th-century documents, the terms *relatively stable* or even *somewhat stable* proved to be exaggerations. There are a core quantity of words within these analyzed documents that are either fairly stable or have only one or two variations. Nevertheless, there are still an abundance of words whose spelling could only be described as extremely erratic. Overriding any unsettling characteristics, however, is the definite existence in many of these documents of a general drift towards standardization.[31]

SOME OF THE MANY WORDS THAT SHOWED SIGNS OF STABILIZING AT THE END OF THE MIDDLE-ENGLISH PERIOD	
PREFERRED SPELLING	VARIATIONS BEING SLOWLY ELIMINATED
also	alsoo, all so, al soe
made	maad, maade, mad
after	aftir, aftur, aftre
this	thys, þis, yis
for	ffor, fore, fo

This stabilizing spelling system originated in the offices of the Royal Chancery. Its emergence and development within that government department can be seen by viewing the transcribed documents in *An Anthology of Chancery English* (1984). On page 27 of that publication the authors make this statement: "The Chancery clerks fairly consistently preferred the spellings which have since become standard....At the very least, we can say that they were trying to limit choices among spellings, and that by the 1440's and 1450's they had achieved a comparative regularization." Clearly, the extremely influential government scribes of late Middle English were starting to get their ink-dippin', quill-pushin', letter-placin' acts together.

Unfortunately, the Middle-English period ended before this stabilizing spelling system had a chance to have much of an influence on lesser scribes. Or to achieve — even in the hands of the better scribes — the rigidity or national uniformity we have today. It was, however, on the right track.

Part Of A Royal Chancery Document (1449)[32]

(Typical late Middle-English stabilizing spelling.
Inconsistent spelling on this page has been underlined.
Notice the letter þ (thorn) is still in use. þ = th)

The kyng by þaduise and assent of the lordes spirituell and
temporell beyng in this present parlement woll and grauntith
þat þe saide Sir Iohn Talbot haue and occupie the saide
office of Chaunceller of Irelond by hym self or by his
sufficient depute there after the fourme of the kynges lettres
patentes to hym made þerof. the whiche lettres patentes byn
thought gode and effectuell and to be approved after the
tenure of the same Also þat þe grete seal of þe saide lond
belongyng to þe saide office. Which þe said Thomas hath
geton vn to hym be delyuered to þe said Sir Iohn Talbot. or
to his sufficiante depute hauyng power of hym to resceiue
hit. And þat þe said Sir Iohn Talbot. haue bothe writtes and
priue seals. such and als many as byn behovefull and
necessarie for hym. als well to þe lieutenant of Irlond or his
depute. and þe Counseill þere to do restore the said Sir Iohn
Talbot vn to þe said office. and hym to putte in pesible
possession of þe same: To haue and to occupie after the
tenure of his said lettres patentes. as to the said Thomas
chargyng hym vppon his ligeaunce for to restore and
delyuere þe said seall to þe said Sir Iohn Talbot after þe
tenure of his said supplicacion any lettres patentes made to
the said Thomas of þe said office in that partie notte with
stondyng. And as teuchyng the remenaunt that ys desired
by this peticion the kyng will be aduysed.

33

So now we have the second stabilizing period. Was it good? No. It was better than the much more diverse previous period, yes, but it still wasn't good. God is good, sex is good (especially when it's sinful), but the stabilizing spelling system used by the best scribes in this period could only be described as marginally tolerable. Its finest characteristic was that it was heavily influenced by the dialect of the greater London area. This meant — even though it was probably unintentional — that it was suited to the largest concentration of people in the country. It would make even more sense today since greater London is expanding so fast that by the year 2050 it is expected to have suburbs in northern Scotland and international fishing rights on mainland Europe.

Counteracting this reasonable characteristic, however, was the influence of dialects from other regions and the integration of traditions from other times. What really moved this system away from being tolerable, all the same, was the powerful attraction it had toward spelling like the French again. This latest layering of French flavoring basically came about because royal scribes had been writing in French for over 350 years and people with traditions that old weren't about to change their spelling habits just because the language they were writing in was new.

Despite these negative features, one book on the subject of spelling says that English spelling in this period was heading towards being phonetic again.[33] Another goes as far as to say it was relatively phonetic already.[34] Unfortunately, though, the word *phonetic* means different things to different people. And so, incidentally, does the word *relatively*. For example, I'm relatively sure that spelling was relatively phonetic at this time (using some far-fetched definition of the word phonetic). However, with the French spelling conventions being used alongside the English ones, and with the influence of dialects and traditions from different regions and times, and with the inconsistency that was still abundant in this system, I'm also relatively sure that all the nasty things I said about the last period still apply here. Except maybe with a little less venom.

Yes, the stabilizing spelling used by the best scribes at this time was obviously better than the heightened instability of the previous period, that's for sure. But so what — it still wasn't good. As I was saying, God is good, sex is good (especially when it's bad). Good is passing your driving test with flying colors. In my opinion, though, this spelling system is the equivalent of making it around the test route without killing pedestrians.

Here endeth the Middle-English period, with a whimper. English gradually became the written language of government again and spelling (at least in the hands of the better scribes) became slightly more stable because of it. Nothing else happened in this period worth writing home about. Once we move ahead to Modern English, all the same, there's a bottomless pit of incomprehensibly thick-witted things for the irreverent at heart to gripe about. If you think our spelling has been made unnecessarily complex up to now — you ain't seen nothing yet!

36

Modern English

Chapter 7
15TH-CENTURY RELATIVELY MINOR DESTABILIZATION (THE CENTURY OF WILLIAM CAXTON)

In the 76th year of the 15th century, which is a fancy way of saying 1476, a man named William Caxton brought the printing press to Britain. This marked the beginning of the changeover from manuscripts being individually handwritten by scribes to books and other documents being mechanically mass-produced by printers. It also marked the beginning of the end of all hope for our spelling.

Some say Caxton and the early printers simply copied the spelling conventions of the scribes in this period. Others say Caxton and his followers went a little further and advanced whatever stability the scribes already had. On the other hand, many say Caxton and the early printers cast our spelling into confusion.[35] Which is true? A little of each again? Probably. After studying the surviving evidence, however, the following points become clear.

If Caxton and his fellow printers copied the conventions of the scribes, it was *all* the scribes they copied — the best, the worst, and the vastly varied in-between. If Caxton and his followers helped stabilization, it was mostly the alphabet they helped stabilize when they started to eliminate the letters *thorn* (þ) and *yogh* (ȝ), because these letters posed problems for their primitive printing presses. Or it was the letters they helped stabilize when they made every letter *a* look exactly like every other letter *a* in their paragraphs and pages. What Caxton and his immediate sidekicks probably did not do, though (according to a number of well-respected experts), was stabilize or advance the stabilization of spelling. "On the contrary," as N.F. Blake says in *Caxton and His World*, "there is much to suggest that at first the printing press led to variety rather than uniformity."[36]

Caxton himself was heavily influenced by the immensely varied spellings in all the different manuscripts he duplicated. He even copied some spellings from foreign manuscripts he translated, for heaven's sake.[37] Furthermore, when uninfluenced by a document he is said to have ad-libbed his spelling or used forms from his youth in England or his adult life abroad, which were out of step with his place and time.[38] Specifically, Caxton's printed works are credited with being the first instances in English where the word *ghost* appears with its characteristic silent *h*. Although Caxton's influence seems to have had a lasting effect on at least this one spelling, overall his diverse and extremely inconsistent and erratic behavior was probably not the quintessential source of our eventual stability.

In this chapter, whenever I talk about Caxton's spelling or other printers' spelling, I'm generally talking about the spelling that came from their printing presses. Most printers, even in the early years, had typesetters setting up the words on their printing presses for them. This means the spelling that came from the early printing presses was often influenced — among many other things — by the spelling habits of these typesetters.

As previously mentioned, there were many dialects in England in the 15th century. Caxton, like the better scribes that went before him, chose to use the dialect of London for his publications. This improved his spelling within certain bounds by eliminating a number of regional variations and by narrowing his phonetic choices. It also automatically brought his spelling closer to the spelling of the better scribes. This does not mean, however, that Caxton necessarily favored the spelling of these scribes. Or that his spelling showed any of the tendencies towards standardization that theirs did.[39]

Robert A. Peters, author of *A Linguistic History of English*, helps confirm Caxton's lack of standardization when he writes: "in Caxton's works the following variants for 'French' occur: ffrensh, frensh, frenssh, frenshe, frensshe, ffrensshe, ffrenshe, Frensshe, Frenshe."[40] This is like Aussie-rules football — anything goes.

Professor D.G. Scragg verifies that the example given in that last quotation isn't an isolated case designed to annoy the French, when he says: "Consistency in the spelling of individual words, which had been achieved by the best London scribes of [Caxton's] day, is noticeably lacking in his work."[41] *I'll* say it's noticeably lacking. Nine variants for one word is definitely not *consistency in the spelling of individual words*. (Eight is the cut-off point in any rulebook I've ever seen.) Obviously, Caxton's spelling didn't just differ from the best scribes' spelling. On a regular basis it differed from his own, too.

A Page From The Prologue Of William Caxton's Translation Of *Eneydos* (1490)[42]

(Caxton's inconsistent spelling on this page has been underlined. In this passage Caxton is talking about the dialect variations in England during his time)

fayn wolde I satysfye euery man / and so to doo toke an olde boke and redde therin / and certaynly the englysshe was so rude and brood that I coude not wele vnderstande it. And also my lorde abbot of westmynster ded do shewe to me late certayn euydences wryton in olde englysshe for to reduce it in to our englysshe now vsid / And certaynly it was wreton in suche wyse that it was more lyke to dutche than englysshe I coude not reduce ne brynge it to be vnderstonden / And certaynly our langage now vsed varyeth ferre from that. whiche was vsed and spoken whan I was borne / For we englysshe men / ben borne vnder the domynacyon of the mone. whiche is neuer stedfaste / but euer wauerynge / wexynge one season / and waneth & dyscreaseth another season / And that comyn englysshe that is spoken in one shyre varyeth from a nother. In so moche that in my dayes happened that certayn marchauntes were in a shippe in tamyse for to haue sayled ouer the see into zelande / and for lacke of wynde thei taryed atte forlond. and wente to lande for to refreshe them And one of theym named sheffelde a mercer cam in to an hows and axed for mete. and specyally he axyd after egges And the goode wyf answerde. that she coude speke no frensshe. And the marchaunt was angry. for he also coude speke no frensshe. but wolde haue hadde egges / and she vnderstode hym not / And thenne at laste a nother sayd that he wolde haue eyren / then the good wyf sayd that she vnderstod hym wel / Loo what sholde a man in thyse dayes now wryte. egges or eyren / certaynly it is harde to playse euery man / by cause of dyuersite & chaunge of langage. For in these dayes euery man that is in ony reputacyon in his countre. wyll vtter his commynycacyon and maters in suche maners & termes / that fewe men shall vnderstonde theym / And som ho-

Because of the above information and because I took a comprehensive look at how Caxton and his followers spelled, I am forced to the following conclusion. When Caxton purchased his printing press, the salesperson omitted to tell him that the changes he guaranteed the machine would bring were supposed to be changes for the better. Consequently, Caxton helped bestow upon us the third and final (albeit relatively minor) destabilization period in this version of the history of English spelling.[43] Amazingly, Caxton committed this crime in broad daylight, because unlike the destabilization in the middle of the Old-English period, or the destabilization in the middle of the Middle-English period, the destabilization that Caxton is accused of creating didn't occur in the *dark ages* this time — even though one look at his spelling might lead you to believe it did.

A FEW OF THE HUNDREDS OF VARIATIONS IN SPELLING FOUND IN JUST ONE OF CAXTON'S PRINTED BOOKS	
MODERN-DAY SPELLING	SOME OF CAXTON'S VARIATIONS
through	thurgh, thorugh, thorowe
sword	swerd, swerde, suerd
realm	realme, reame, reaume
said	saide, sayde, seid
more	more, moo, mo

See endnote[44]

It is entirely possible that Caxton knew nothing about the slightly more consistent spelling of the better scribes. After all, he had been trained in spelling early in the 15th century, had been out of the country since then and missed all the updates. Furthermore, the typesetters he hired to help him wouldn't have been able to help him in this regard because they had been out of the country even longer than he had. In fact, they had never been in it before. They were foreigners — foreigners who knew precious little English. So it's a sure bet if they didn't know much English, their understanding of the scribal-spelling traditions wouldn't have been up to snuff either.

The other printing shops that soon sprouted up to exploit this new medium of printing had the good sense to employ English-born typesetters. Even they didn't seem to know about the more consistent spelling of the better scribes, though, because they developed their own irregular systems, independent of these scribes. And often independent of Caxton, his helpers, and each other too.[45] These typesetters were given few or no rules to follow when it came to spelling, and it showed. Thank Heavens we don't spell today like they did.

Wait a minute. On occasion, I do spell like they did. Obviously in a past life I used to be someone from that time. Today, because of my imperfect spelling abilities, I'm not even considered proficient enough to write a memo. Back then, however, I could have been a typesetter, or even a publisher like Caxton. Incredible. There but for the disgrace of spelling, go I.

43

As I said, it is possible that Caxton knew nothing about the more consistent spelling of the better scribes, although in my estimation, that is extremely unlikely.[46] Caxton was a very smart, well-read multilinguist, so I'm sure he was aware of the spelling conventions of not only the best scribes but the best scribes in many different countries. He was also renowned for his sense of humor, though, so there's a further possibility his spelling was a practical joke on us.

Anything's possible, but on reflection, I doubt that too, because Caxton was first and foremost a businessman — one who had proven himself by making a fortune abroad in the textile industry. So I'm sure that any decisions he made were based solely on profit-oriented principles, not on whether he'd get a laugh from them or not.

Nobody is sure why Caxton spelled the way he did (or spelled the way he didn't, depending on how you look at it). This leaves the door wide open for my imagination to run wild again. At first I thought Caxton adopted his sloppy spelling system because it was simply cheaper to use than a more stable one. After all, there was no time or money wasted resetting type to correct spelling mistakes. All he had to do was make sure his words were in the correct order, and that, in turn, would make his lines come out right — especially the bottom one. It just made good business sense not to worry about spelling.

Then I thought, maybe Caxton and the other printers were simply following the time-honored business philosophy of giving the public what it wanted. Since the public didn't know what it wanted, the printers obliged by giving it something equally as vague in response to the public demand.

Finally I thought, to heck with all this speculation. If in a past life I really did live in Caxton's time (as my spelling suggests), why don't I just hypnotize myself, regress to that former existence, and talk to Caxton myself. So that's exactly what I did. And what do you know — it worked. (Things always work out when a wild imagination is used.)

Some of what Caxton and I talked about is private because it's boring and doesn't make good reading. The remainder is printed below for all to see. And for all to make up their minds whether it should have been private, too.

Niall: "Tell me, Mr. Caxton, what's your excuse for having so many different spellings for the same words?"

Caxton: "Well, Niall...may I call you Niall?"

Niall: "Sure, but you're saying it wrong. It should be sounded like *meal*. It's the Celtic spelling of *Neil*."

Caxton: "Very good. By the way, *Niall*, has anyone ever pointed out that maybe the reason you can't spell is because some nincompoop spelled your name wrong at birth?"

Niall: "You're only the millionth person to suggest that."

Caxton: "Yes, well, it's good to know so many people agree with me. Now where were we? Ah, yes. Why the varied spelling? It's simple really. I had a choice. I could have given each word only one spelling and everything I printed would have been uniform and page-like, just like your modern reading material. Alternatively, I could have varied my spelling to make everything I printed look much less like text and much more like patterned lines. After much deliberation, I settled on the printing that looked more liked patterned lines so I could print it on cloth and sell it as the latest style in fabric, just in case the sale of printed books didn't go as well as planned."

Niall: "How very crafty of you, Mr. Caxton. For some reason, I get the impression you might have enjoyed printing words on cloth even more than printing them on paper."

Caxton: "You're right. Apart from the money I could have made, just think how perfect a prank it would have been: Even though people wouldn't have known it, they'd be right up to the minute in both the clothing and the writing styles! Moreover, whether they wanted to or not, they'd be making both a fashion and a written statement!"

Niall: "Ha, ha. Very droll, Mr. Caxton. Some of that famous Caxton humor, I imagine."

So there we have it. The rationale of a textile merchant for possibly causing as much disruption to our spelling system as any of the excitement-seeking monks or priests that came before him. Or, as Mr. Caxton with his renowned sense of jest might have put it, "the spelling system was disrupted once again by yet another man of the cloth."

ALTERNATIVE THEORY

As mentioned at the start of this chapter, some people have the opinion that Caxton and the early printers advanced whatever stability the scribes already had. If we compare Caxton's and the early printers' spelling to the spelling of *all* scribes (from the best to the worst), there's a possibility that this hypothesis could be true. If, however, we compare the spelling of Caxton and his followers only to the spelling of the *best* scribes (like I and others have done), the likelihood diminishes considerably.

This is not to say, however, that we should completely dismiss the possibility that Caxton and his print-mates slightly improved things. On the contrary, there is always the potential when new evidence develops or when further analysis is performed, that fresh insight will enlighten us to a more complete understanding of this situation. Fresh insight, after all, has altered people's opinions on this particular debate for decades: one book says one thing is true, another book with fresher insight says the opposite; a third with even newer information agrees with the first; and a fourth with the very latest interpretation lines up with the second. Back and forth, forth and back, for at least 30 years.[47] Indeed, the debate will assuredly continue — in both directions — for many more decades to come.

Even if it turns out (after all the evidence is in) that the spelling of Caxton and the early printers *is* considered to be slightly better than that of the best scribes, I will still be compelled to call William Caxton a destabilizer because his and the early printers' spelling did not replace scribal spelling — *it was added to it!* Both systems traveled side by side for many decades after the introduction of printing. Sometimes they ignored each other (and followed their own whims), and other times they influenced each other (and followed each others whims). Either way, they were both part of the mainstream-spelling package of that day. Alone, each was bad enough. Together, they helped create the irritatingly unstable spelling of the late 15th century, which ultimately led to the irritatingly stable spelling we have today.

Along with traveling side-by-side with scribal spelling (and the many other things I have mentioned), here are three further reasons why Caxton's and the early printers' spelling was probably more disruptive than that of the better scribes. First, the printers, unlike the scribes, arbitrarily changed the spelling of their words when their rinky-dink printing presses ran out of letters. Second, the printers, unlike the scribes, equalized the length of their printed lines by varying the spelling of their words. Third, the printers, unlike the scribes, had immense reproduction capabilities, so when Caxton and the early printers varied the spelling of their words, these variations were repeated *over* and *ovir* and *ovyr* again. The net result being, we received in the late 15th century some of the most repetitive, chaotic spelling we've ever had.

Chapter 8
16TH-CENTURY TRAUMATIZATION
& RE-EMERGING STABILIZATION
(THE CENTURY OF THE PRINTER)

In the 16th century, with absolutely no prompting from me, the printers finally came to their senses and became increasingly influenced by the better scribes. This brought a great deal of stability to our spelling, especially in the second half of the century. Despite this improvement, though, the following five *Traumatic Spelling Disturbances*, which happened around this time, will help explain why I consider spelling to have remained in a considerable amount of flux right to the very end of this century. These disturbances aren't the sole possession of the 16th century. Some of them started before it began and others remained after it ended. Nevertheless, I've placed them here because this is where they did most of their damage — and what better place to hold them accountable for their actions than at the scene of their worst crimes.

TRAUMATIC DISTURBANCE # 1:
THE BUDDY SYSTEM

The Buddy System is, as my name for it implies, a situation in which two or more typesetters worked together on the same printed book. This isn't an unusual occurrence, I'm sure it goes on even today, but today our spelling is stable and all typesetters working on the same book spell the same way, so it's harder to detect. Back in the 16th century, however, spelling was a lot more flexible and all typesetters, to differing degrees, spelled their own way. This often included following the irregular spelling of the manuscripts they were copying, a freedom in the spelling of vowel sounds, and it always included the use of variants. So, with two or more typesetters doing all these different things on the same book, no one should be shocked to learn it was normal to find a number of different spellings for the same word on the same page. I'm just surprised that any word was ever spelled the same way twice!

Some would say that this common practice of mixing the spelling habits of two or more typesetters within individual books would make the spelling of the 16th century appear worse than it actually was. As the great singer/songwriter, Kris Kristofferson, once said, though, "If it sounds country, man, that's what it is." If the spelling of the 16th century looked irregular, man, then that's what it was, because it was the combination of all the irregularities that the book-buying public had to deal with, not just the limited instability of one individual typesetter.

TRAUMATIC DISTURBANCE # 2:
LINE JUSTIFICATION

Line justification occurs when the right-hand end of lines of text on a printed page are made to line up with each other, just like the left-hand ends do. The result of this is a uniform page where most of the lines of text are of equal length. It's an aesthetic feature that is easily achieved today with the electronic spacing ability of computers. This spacing ability, however, was not one that the early printers, with their hand-operated screw-presses, possessed. Therefore, when they came to justify their lines, they did it in many instances by varying the spelling of their words. If they could find commonly used variants of the right length, then they'd use them. If they couldn't, though, they'd just add or subtract a couple of letters to or from as many words as was necessary to make their lines come out even.

A Justified Paragraph From Page 14
Of Angel Day's *The English Secretorie* (1586)[48]
(The second underlined word is an example
of respelling for justification purposes)

In lightnesse or grauitie of a man, we shall chiefly have regard to his aucthoritie or profession, for neyther all thinges to all men are conuenient, nor one thing to e-uery man may easily be adapted. In one kinde wee frame our letters to olde men, in an other sorte to <u>young</u>, one way to sad and graue persons, an other to light or <u>yong</u> fellowes, one platforme to Courtiers, an other to Philo-sophers.

Up to this moment in my life, I have always thought that all people were created equal. It's obvious to me now, though, that the early printers must have swung from a different branch of the evolutionary tree than the rest of us, because even the worst scribes didn't justify like that. Initially, I figured the scribes wouldn't need to, since they had the flexibility of hand writing to stretch words out like mozzarella from a pizza. In general, however, they didn't do that either. Instead, they simply finished their lines off at the last reasonably spelled word that came close to their right hand margin. Then, on occasion, they filled in the gap (if there was one) with a variety of different-shaped markings. This seems like a reasonably sane method to me. So sane, in fact, that to begin with the printers actually used it. Before long, though, someone came up with the spelling-variation idea and the printers jumped on it like it was a band wagon and they were the trumpet section.

On account of all the other goofing around that was going on at the same time, it is fairly difficult to pinpoint the actual words we have today that were directly affected by line justification. Many experts say, however, that at least some of the confusion in our spelling today was caused by that activity — and who am I to argue with these experts, especially when they're agreeing with me?[49]

A dumb thing like justification on its own, with its limited effect on our spelling system, isn't that terrible. Nevertheless, when it's added to the accumulation of irregularities mentioned in the previous chapters and when it is realized that a great many people today want to keep all these irregularities because they think they look good, then it's more obvious how bad things really are. It's also more obvious, because of this information, that maybe it wasn't just the early printers who swung from a different branch of the evolutionary tree. Maybe all the people who want to keep our spelling the way it is swung from that same branch too — and landed on their heads. The larger brains that some of them think they have is undoubtedly from the swelling.

Purely for my own understanding, let me run through this once more. Because of justification, we made some words longer for the aesthetics of the lines, and now, because we're used to these and other words being longer, we keep them longer for the aesthetics of the words, even though we sometimes have to hyphenate these words because they're now too long to fit on the end of some of our lines. Yep, just as I thought — it makes no sense. And to think all the other animals on the planet let us run the world because we're supposed to be the smartest. Obviously, we're dumber than they think.

TRAUMATIC DISTURBANCE # 3:
THE RENAISSANCE

Amazingly enough, while this sorry excuse for a spelling system was in its heyday, so in England was the third major disturbance, the Renaissance. I say "amazingly enough" because of the contrast. The Renaissance was the rebirth of culture and learning that swept over most of Europe in and around this time. It was an explosion of inspiration that left in its path great discoveries in science, magnificent masterpieces in literature, and works of art the likes of which had never been seen before. Meanwhile, there our spelling system was at the other extreme, with its pathetically primitive variability. It's obvious from this that spelling's rebirth peaked too early with the best scribes at the end of the Middle-English period and what the late 15th and Early 16th century got was the placenta.

This pathetic spelling was upon us while Sir Thomas More, the English author, was writing *Utopia* and while Nicolaus Copernicus, the Polish astronomer, was convincing us the earth went round the sun (instead of the other way around as we thought before).

It was also upon us, I must add, while Leonardo da Vinci, the Italian inventor and painter, was creating the likes of the *Mona Lisa*. So now, finally, after years of speculation by others, I may have found the real reason for Mona's muted smile. Leonardo was asking her not to grin because he couldn't do teeth, while at the same time he was telling her English spelling jokes!

The following I'm sure was one of his favorites: "How many Englishmen does it take to light a candle? Seventeen; one to hold the candle, one to ignite the wick, and fifteen to decipher the instructions." Another of his favorites must have been, "What do you call a 300-pound Englishman who claims that English spelling is phonetic? Anything you like; he can't hear you." This next one I'm sure Mona would have loved. "What do you call a seven-foot Englishman who spells his name the same

52

way three times in a row? Sir, because the Queen has knighted him for his intellectualism." Not exactly prime-time television material; but with the correct media hype, laugh track, and a few examples of 16th-century English spelling, it could be.

The irregularity and variability of 16th-century English spelling was clearly disruptive. Nevertheless, it's the foreign words that entered English in and around this period that have elevated the Renaissance to the level of *Traumatic Spelling Disturbance*. One or two foreign words wouldn't have hurt, but literally thousands of them from a multitude of different languages became English at this time. Words flowed in from Greek, French, Italian, Spanish, and even some originally derived from Hebrew and Arabic. Over 50 languages made contributions to English before the Renaissance was over.[50] Many languages only contributed a few words, but one tongue, Latin, caused more than its fair share of trouble because the largest portion of new words came from that one language alone.

A SMALL SAMPLE OF THE LARGE NUMBER OF LATIN WORDS THAT ENTERED ENGLISH DURING THE RENAISSANCE		
MODERN-DAY ENGLISH SPELLING	LATIN SPELLING BEFORE ENTRY INTO ENGLISH	16TH-CENTURY ENGLISH VARIANTS
education	educationem	educacion, educatyon, education
extinguish	exstinguere	extynguysh, extynguish, extinguishe
sincere	sincerus	sincer, sinceir, syncere
fascinate	fascinatus	fascinate, fascynate, fascinat
deficient	deficientem	deficient, defycient, defycyent

This massive influx of Latin words came about because, along with the great strides into the future that people experienced during the Renaissance, giant steps were also taken back into the past to study the teachings of ancient civilizations. During these intellectual excursions, scholars went gaga over Latin and borrowed words from it freely.

Latin admiration didn't stop at the borrowing of words, though. It extended to everything about the language. As a matter of fact, Latin was held in such high regard in the 16th century that heated battles often raged between rival intellectuals to determine which should be the language of learning, English or Latin. English won, of course, although it's sometimes hard to tell because Latin didn't just give us bundles of new words to wrestle with. It also gave us new ways to spell many of our old words. It must have been a compromise between the opposing learned factions: "Right then, we'll use English, but we'll pepper it up with so much Latin memorabilia that it will still feel like we're learning in Latin. And, more importantly, it will make English much more difficult for lower-class plebes to master."

SOME OF THE MANY ENGLISH WORDS INFLUENCED BY LATIN SPELLING DURING THE RENAISSANCE			
MODERN-DAY ENGLISH SPELLING	INFLUENTIAL LATIN SPELLING	COMMON ENGLISH VARIANT BEFORE LATIN INFLUENCE	16TH-CENTURY ENGLISH VARIANTS AFTER LATIN INFLUENCE (SOME ARE UNINFLUENCED)
schedule	schedula	sedule	schedule, schedull, schedul
phlegm	phlegma	fleme	phlegm, phlegme, phleugme
rhyme	rhythmus	ryme	rhyme, rhime, rime
subtle	subtilis	sutil	subtle, sotell, suttle
anchor	anchora	ancre	achor, anchor, ancour

See endnote [51]

Perhaps I'm being too cynical. Maybe the people of the Renaissance simply Latinized their spelling so they could be more like the ancient civilizations they admired so much. If that was the case, though, why didn't they just have wild drunken orgies with their mothers and sisters, like the Romans did, or worship gods who were once people? At least that kind of mimicry is only recorded in history books, not dictionaries and spelling books.

An excuse that is often given for the Latinization of spelling at this time is that classical Latin spelling was stable and English spelling of the renaissance wasn't. This is supposed to have caused renaissance scholars to spell English words the stable Latin way. Forgive my criticism, but why go back to ancient times to a language far removed from their own when they could have created stability by picking and choosing spellings that still resembled *English* right in their own tongue?

In addition to the reasons already given, one other possible explanation for 16th-century Latinization warrants exploration, because if it turns out to be true it will be the dumbest distortion that's ever happened to our spelling. Maybe even the dumbest thing that's ever happened to anything anywhere. Before dealing with this in detail, though, first a little background.

According to professor D.G. Scragg, in France in the Middle Ages, Latinized spellings, because they were generally longer, "were particularly favored in legal language, because lawyers' clerks were paid for writing by the inch and superfluous letters provided a useful source of income."[52] Let me say that a different way, because it just doesn't sound as bad as it really is. For every inch of writing the French legal clerks wrote, they were paid a certain amount of money for it. Holy socks! That's not exactly what I call an incentive for brevity. In fact, I'm sure these clerks went to great lengths to find the spellings that would stretch these documents out as long as possible. Personally, I'd have used the mozzarella method that everyone seems to be avoiding, but I guess these clerks, being of the legal profession, had higher moral standards than I have. Either that or being of the legal profession they realized their method was a much more honest way of robbing people.

Now for the foreground. I searched and searched, but nowhere could I specifically find that long *Latinized* spellings were used in 16th-century England by legal clerks who were trying to increase their income. I did, however, find that extra letters were placed in words, huge margins were created, and lines were spaced ridiculously far apart by lawyers and clerks who were paid by the length of their documents.[53] I also found that no matter how many rules were set up to try to stop this abuse, these professional loop-holers would always find new and ingenious ways to get around them. So, given this information and my previous account of the number of Latinized words that entered English during the Renaissance, I personally don't think it's too wild of me to assume that some of that ingenuity came in the form of long Latinized words and spellings. Even if it *is* too much to assume, it is clear to me that spelling in this period was still affected by elongated Latinization caused by the legal profession, because some of the French words that entered English back in Middle English were already contaminated by this phenomenon before we got them. Therefore, this is not probably — it's *definitely* the dumbest thing that's ever happened to our spelling.

TRAUMATIC DISTURBANCE # 4: FALSE ETYMOLOGY

When a person investigates and traces the origin and development of a word, that field of study is called etymology. When that person takes that studied word and changes its modern spelling to bring it closer into line with its ancient spelling, that, quite frankly, has got to be categorized as just plain dopey. Despite its obvious regressiveness, though, that's the kind of thing that was done to our spelling in and around this time. This was done not only to words of Latin origin (as mentioned in the previous disturbance) but also to words of Greek, French, Old English, and many other origins. Essentially, someone would trace the ancestry of a word, pick one or two letters from the ancient or older foreign spelling of that word, and insert them into our more modern version. These new letters often remain silent in our language despite the fact they were usually never silent in the original language they came from.

As if this is not ridiculous enough, we also have words in our language that had letters inserted into them based on false or incorrect etymology. That is, someone wrongly assumed the origin of a word and based on that incorrect assumption changed our more modern spelling accordingly. For example, in middle and early Modern English, *island*, a word that came to us from Old English, was happily going on its way using spellings like *iland* and *yland*. Then in the 16th century, scholars incorrectly concluded that *island* had come to us from the Latin word *insula*, and inserted the erroneous silent *s*.

The spelling of *could* is even more outrageous. This word came to us from the Old-English word *cuðe*. It was spelled *coud* and *coude* in early Modern English. It was soon changed when scholars decided it should have a silent *l* like *would* and *should*, since all three came to us from Old English. The only trouble is, *would* and *should* actually had *l* sounds in them in Old English — *could* never did.

Scissors is another example. In the late 15th century, this word had no trouble surviving with a simple *s* or a less-simplistic *c* at the beginning (e.g., *sisours, sysors, cysors, cysars,* etc.) The *c* spellings were based on relatively sound reasoning since *scissors* came to us through the Old-French word *cisoires*, from the Latin *cisorium*. The *s* spellings, on the other hand, were our futile attempts to spell the word the way it sounds in English. In the 16th century, however, misguided individuals (realizing we weren't experiencing enough confusion) decided we should use the *s* and *c* together at the beginning of the word. They did this because they thought *scissors* was derived from the Latin word *scissor* — which it wasn't. Although it certainly looks as if it was now.

These false-etymology changes, and a few others in words such as *forei(g)n, g(u)ilt, s(c)ent* and *deli(gh)t,* are what I would call world-class spelling mistakes.[54] The mistakes others and I used to make in school shrivel into oblivion by comparison. And ours were probably more historically correct. When kids create spelling errors in class they are often chastised by their teachers and ridiculed by their peers. Yet scholars and dictionary makers initiated and perpetuated many of the ridiculous mistakes I have listed and they were often assumed to be master etymologists and expert dictionary compilers — both of whom pride themselves in their ability to trace the origin of words. What the heck is wrong with this picture?

TRAUMATIC DISTURBANCE # 5:
THE GREAT VOWEL SHIFT

Over and above all the things I've mentioned, one more unsettling ingredient made the spelling of the 16th century much worse than it should have been: the Great Vowel Shift. The Great Vowel Shift was a phenomenon that caused a major change in the way the English people pronounced their words. It actually occurred over a 200-or-so-year period starting about the year 1400.[55] Nevertheless, it is most significant to us here in the 16th century because this is where we can first look (with safety glasses and a hard hat) at a major part of its destructive effect.

The Great Vowel Shift was an alteration in the way the English pronounce their long vowels that eventually affected the way they say some of their short vowels and even a few of their diphthongs. (A diphthong is a compound vowel sound like the *ou* in *ouch* and the *oi* in *boink*.)

Linguists are not altogether clear why the Great Vowel Shift happened, but it is well documented that it did happen. There is also lots of evidence to suggest that most of the sound changes followed a relatively organized pattern, with many of the affected vowels having their sounds raised to higher positions of articulation in the mouth.

This means that instead of the English people saying the long vowel sound *a*, which is pronounced low in the mouth, they began to say the long vowel sound *e* which is higher. Instead of saying the long vowel sound *e* they started to say the diphthong *i* (ah-ee), since there was no higher position to go to. It was a chain reaction with one vowel sound bumping the sound above it into a new location. Prior to the Great Vowel Shift the *i* in a word like *line* would have sounded something like the *ea* in *lean*, and the *ee* in a word like *feet* would have sounded something like the *a* in *fate*.

Although the Great Vowel Shift may seem like a terrible thing to have happened to the English language, it wouldn't have caused us much trouble at all if English spelling had gone against its natural instinct and *uniformly* changed to suit the new sounds. Further trouble could have been avoided if all the vowel sounds that changed *always* changed in *every* word, and if all the changes were uniform throughout England.

Unfortunately, though, there wasn't this desired level of consistency. Some words changed to suit the new sounds, but most words didn't. Some words received new sounds, but other words didn't. Some words acquired several sounds, and many words with single sounds ended up with several spellings. Furthermore, some vowels under certain circumstances took on sounds that were pronounced lower in the mouth. In summation, the Great Vowel Shift caused a mess that should have been cleaned up with a Pooper-Scooper, but wasn't.

That, my fellow English-speakers, is one of the reasons why in the English language today we have vast quantities of words with mixed-up vowel sounds. The words *flood* and *steak* and *brew* are good examples. If these words were sounded out by people who don't know them, these same people still wouldn't know these words even after they've sounded them out. They would, however, probably know the sound of a few Swahili words with similar spellings.

SOME OF THE STRANGE VOWEL SPELLINGS CREATED OR ENCOURAGED BY THE GREAT VOWEL SHIFT	
STRANGE VOWEL SPELLING	MODERN-DAY SPELLINGS OF SOME OF THE AFFECTED WORDS
oo-spelling for ŭ-sound	flood, blood
o-spelling for oo-sound	do, to, lose
a-spelling for ŏ-sound	all, salt, malt
ew-spelling for oo-sound	dew, lewd, shrewd
ea-spelling for ā-sound	great, break, steak

See endnote [56]

In essence, then, what we had during the Great Vowel Shift (not counting the African-language lessons) was a situation in which our spelling not only moved away from the sounds of words, as was often the case in the past, but the sound of words also moved away from our spelling. This left us in some cases with an even larger gap between sound and spelling than ever could have been achieved with the old one-directional method of destruction. Proof once again that the more advanced a society is, the more efficient it becomes at doing things badly.

Imagine living in the 16th century with the Great Vowel Shift and all the other Traumatic Spelling Disturbances going on simultaneously. They had multiple typesetters with personal variations, line justification, false etymology, foreign words and influence from Greek, Latin, and scores of other languages, arbitrary elongation of words for extra pocket change, freedom of vowel sounds, variants, and — to top things off — very few rules to guide them along the way.

On the bright side, though, it must have been easy to spell, especially in the more traumatic first half of the 16th century, because so much seemed to be acceptable. I'm willing to bet, however, that reading — or at least attempting to read — must have been the leading cause of illiteracy.

63

THE END OF THE 16TH CENTURY

In the second half of the 16th century, especially toward the end, spelling became a lot more stable. Despite this improvement, though, there was still an abundance of printing shops that had few or no rules for their typesetters to follow. Not surprisingly, there was still a profusion of typesetters who didn't follow any rules. It seems the only objective of these printing shops was to get their shabby product out the door as soon as possible so they could reap the monetary benefits of mass production. Then they'd rush out to buy only quality merchandise for their own consumption with the profits. Good ideas come and go, whereas great business ethics like that seem to last forever.

On the other hand, running parallel with these low-grade unethical printers was a growing number of quality printers who had a little more pride in their work. For a start, they provided guidelines for their employees to follow and, as a result, their spelling is considered by some to have been well on its way to stability. After all is said and done, though, even at the very end of the 16th century, the best of these quality printers still justified by changing the spelling of words and still had a number of typesetters working on the same books with their own personal variations. What's more, the stable spelling of one quality printer wasn't necessarily the same as the stable spelling of another. Call me a skeptic if you will, or even a nitpicker, but it seems to me that even the quality printers could have benefited from a few more guidelines. Not to mention some extra training in letting the left hand know what the right hand was doing.

A Page From William Shakespeare's *Lucrece* (1594) Printed By One Of The Best "Quality Printers" Of The Late 16th Century[57]

(Inconsistent spellings on this page have been underlined.
Words with different spellings on other pages
in the same publication are in bold type)

THE RAPE OF LVCRECE

The **deepe** vexation of his inward soule,
Hath seru'd a **dumbe** arrest **vpon** his **tongue**,
Who mad that sorrow should his use **controll**,
Or **keepe** him from heart-easing words so long,
Begins to talke, but through his lips **do** thron
   Weake words, so thick come in his **poor** harts aid,
   That no man could distinguish what **he said**.

Yet sometime Tarqvin was pronounced plaine,
But through his teeth, as if the name he tore,
This windie tempest, till it blow vp raine,
Held **backe** his sorrowes tide, to make it more.
At last it raines, and busie windes giue ore,
   Then sonne and father **weep** with equall strife,
   Who shuld **weep** most for daughter or for wife.

The one doth call her his, the other his,
Yet neither may possesse the claime they **lay**.
The father saies, shee's mine, o mine **shee** is
Replies her husband, **do** not take **away**
My sorrowes interest, let no mourner **say**
   He weepes for her, for **shee** was onely mine,
   And onelie must be wayl'd by Colatine.

65

To conclude this chapter on a more positive note, the general overall spelling of the quality printers at the end of the 16th century was, as it turns out, more stable than the general overall spelling of the better scribes at the end of the Middle-English period. So the dysfunctional disruption that took place in-between these times, was temporary — at least as far as *stability* is concerned. As far as *complexity* and *confusion* are concerned, the disruption has proven to be much longer lasting. Indeed, on account of what happens in the next period, it has proven to be damned near permanent.

Chapter 9
17TH-CENTURY FINAL STABILIZATION (THE CENTURY OF THE SPELLING BOOK)

This century is subtitled "The Century of the Spelling Book" because I believe a spelling book greatly accelerated the stabilization process during this time span. As I see it, there were three main forces at work on the spelling of the 17th century: the force of the printer, the force of the public, and the force of the spelling book. I suppose any one of these influences could easily be interpreted to be the most important. After all, take any one of them away and 17th-century stabilization as we know it might never have happened. Even so, I still without hesitation choose the spelling book as the most crucial. Because without the spelling book's guidance, the printers might still be only *well on their way to stability* (with all their personal variations) and the public would think that what the printers are doing is right. This would leave us now with what we had in the 16th century, and that would be a disaster. As, in fact, it was.

At about the same time as English spelling was being finally stabilized, another important event in world history was taking place. In 1607 at Jamestown, Virginia, the first successful permanent English colony in North America was established. This early colony was the first of the original 13 colonies that in the late 18th century would form the United States of America.

With the establishment of this first English colony in the New World, English spelling (like many other European diseases and unwelcome creatures) seized its opportunity to perpetrate its peskiness on a new continent. The early American colonists were primarily interested in building their houses, planting their crops, and preparing or recovering from whatever catastrophe might or had befallen them. Simultaneously, however, they also had the need to read and write. This, unfortunately, made spelling unavoidable.

In the 17th century the English colonies of America were just that — *English* colonies. As such, they looked to England for guidance in matters such as government, manners, style, etc. Consequently, there was never any question as to what form of spelling to use — they used the spelling of their British bibles and books, the spelling of their British parents and siblings. They used the spelling they brought from their homeland.[58]

Of course, since British spelling was still in the process of stabilization, the spelling that the colonists used in the 17th century was always slightly behind that of their more up-to-date British cousins. In comparison to the people in Britain, the colonists often used older printed material, and used that material for longer. Newer material and ideas took quite a while to paddle their way across the channel.

The intelligent and resourceful early colonists did not rely solely on British publications for their books and other reading material. In late 1638 or early 1639 they were printing their own stuff. Steven and Matthew Daye — a father and son duo — were America's first printers. These gentlemen lacked the literary vision of England's first printer, Caxton. No Chaucers or Miltons or even Shakespeares emerged from the inked plates of their press (at least while they were using it). Colonial Americans were interested in more practical publications such as almanacs, religious texts, and law books. They needed to know when to plant their crops, what prayers to say to make these crops grow, and who to sue if they didn't grow. In 1643, the Dayes also printed the first spelling book in America. Apparently, early colonial practicality also included knowing precisely where to place highly *impractical* silent and double letters.

The spelling that the Dayes and the few other 17th-century colonial printers used was nothing special. They and the other more literate American colonists of this period essentially used — with a slight delay — the spelling of the British Isles. It wasn't until the late 18th century that being British and following British traditions and guidelines were brought into question, and even then the questions were primarily written using British spelling.

The Cover Page Of An Almanac Printed By
Matthew Daye (1647)[59]

(Typical early colonial printers' spelling. Fundamentally British
spelling with a slight information and time delay. Spellings that
are foreign to us today are underlined. *Almanack, arctick,
colledge,* and *solde* were accepted spellings in Britain in 1647.
Hez(ekiah) Usher was America's first bookseller)

M DC XLVII.

AN

A L M A N A C K
FOR THE YEAR OF OUR
LORD
1647

Calculated for the longitude of 315
degr. and Elevation of the Pole <u>Ar-
ctick</u> 42 degr. & 30 min. & may generally serve for the most part of

New-England.

*By Samuel Danforth of Harvard <u>Colledge</u>
<u>Philomathemat.</u>*

CAMBRIDGE
Printed by *Matthew Day.*
Are to be <u>solde</u> by Hez. Usher at Boston.
1647

It could be assumed that the history of American spelling started at the beginning of the 17th century. A broader look has revealed, however, that up to the 17th century the history of British spelling was also the early history of American spelling. This is true since America inherited, almost intact, the spelling of the British Isles. Even after 1607 there was no great split between the spelling used in Britain and the spelling used in the American colonies. Admittedly, some of the many new words coined or borrowed because of contact with the New World did influence the Old Country and the new colonies in different ways. In general, however, colonial American spelling in the 17th century was still fundamentally guided by the often-goofball antics and events that went on in Britain.

THE THIRD AND FINAL STABILIZATION

During the course of the 17th century, spelling stabilized again for the third and final time. Stabilization was so complete on this occasion that a person reading almost any piece of British or American printed material after the early 18th century would find the spelling not much different from our own.[60] (Which is as good a reason as any for not reading anything past that date. All the good writers had died by then anyway.)

At the start of the 17th century many of the disruptions and disturbances associated with the 16th century were still in existence. By mid-century a sizable amount of that turbulence had subsided and the major part of our stabilization was complete. At the end, apart from some wild capitalization and a few changes to a small number of words to come, we essentially had the advanced prototype for the spelling system we know and love today. Put succinctly, the modern era of stabilized chaos had begun.

A Page From Jonathan Swift's *Gulliver's Travels* (1726)[61]

(Typical early 18th-Century British printers' spelling. Apart from the archaic use of the word *durst*, the spelling on this page was and is correct for both Britain and the United States. The capitalization and general punctuation, however, was still a work in progress)

> I REMEMBER one Morning when *Glumdalclitch* had set me in my box upon a Window, as she usually did in fair Days to give me Air (for I <u>durst</u> not venture to let the Box be hung on a Nail out of the Window, as we do with Cages in *England*) after I had lifted up one of my Sashes, and sat down at my Table to eat a piece of Sweet Cake for my Breakfast, above twenty Wasps, allured by the smell, came flying into the Room, humming louder than the Drones of as many Bagpipes. Some of them seized my Cake, and carried it piece-meal away, others flew about my Head and Face, confounding me with the Noise, and putting me in the utmost terror of their Stings. However I had the Courage to rise and draw my Hanger, and attack them in the Air. I dispatched four of them, but the rest got away, and I presently shut my Window. These Creatures were as large as Partridges, I took out their Stings, found them an Inch and a half long, and as

This third stabilization came about to a large extent because a man in England named Richard Mulcaster inspired another man in England named Edmund Coote to bring out the first comprehensive English spelling book.[62] This book, published in 1596 and still in print 140 years later, was a tremendous success with both the British school system and the British public alike. Its success possibly occurred because Coote was a schoolmaster and his pupils *became* the public, but it more than likely occurred because its title, *The English Schoole-Master*, made everyone think it was a naughty novel with steamy sex scenes: "the English Schoolmaster grabbed the wanton washerwoman firmly by the arm and threw her tenderly down on the bed, etc." (I told you all the good writers were dead.)

The tremendous success of this book (no matter how it came about) meant that now after all this time the public knew exactly what kind of spelling it wanted and the money-loving, business-oriented printers were only too happy to accommodate them. That, in a nutshell, is why the printers of the 17th century eventually stabilized their spelling all in the same public-pleasing, spelling-book-copying way.[63]

The words *stabilized* and *stabilization* conjures up images of uniformity, reliability, and simplicity. Unfortunately, like the previous stabilizations, none of these conjured words even comes close to describing what happened this time. Come to think of it, no words thus far coined in the English language can do that. I'd have to invent my own words to do this phurking rubbish justice.

Coote had the perfect opportunity — a spelling system in turmoil and an educated public ready for change — but he blew it. Instead of devising a nice simplified system of his own creation, or picking the best spellings of the many that were available to him, he picked his spellings, to a noticeable extent, from the variants most frequently in print.[64] That's like choosing an Olympic team from the athletes most frequently at practice. "Okay, John, you're on the relay team, but don't blame me if someone grabs your wooden leg instead of the baton." This is world-class dimwittery. In Coote's defense, though, I have to say that at least by making choices he eliminated a great many variants. I'm not so sure that's something he should be proud of, all the same, because it seems to me he threw away most of the good ones.

A FEW OF THE MANY SPELLINGS CHOSEN BY COOTE THAT HAVE SURVIVED TO THE PRESENT DAY		
MODERN-DAY SPELLING	COOTE'S 1596 SPELLING	OTHER LATE 16TH-CENTURY VARIANTS THAT COOTE COULD HAVE CHOSEN
monarch	monarch	monark, monarke, monarck
receipt	receipt	receit, receite, receate
pigeon	pigeon	pigin, piggen, pigion
rogue	rogue	roge, roag, roage
thyme	thyme	time, tyme, thime

I have suggested that Coote could have abandoned all the spellings that were available to him and devised his own easy-to-learn system, independent of history and tradition. On closer examination, however, I realize the likelihood of him doing that was nil because he was dead-against the wholesale simplification of spelling. He thought it was too unlike the spelling they had back then. He can say that again. Simplified spelling is good, it works, it's easy to learn, and it's sensible — that's nothing like the spelling that existed then.

Coote's concern with simplified spelling being different had very little to do with spelling itself; it had to do with reading. He worried that children who learned simplified spelling at school would have a hard time reading the literature already in print. But surely his choosing the spellings most frequently in print didn't solve that problem. Surely the number of variants in the literature already in print would have meant his students had to skim over words like a flat stone bounces over calm water before they landed on any of *his* spellings. Furthermore, because of the complex spelling in individual words, many kids of this period already had a hard time reading even the most frequent spellings in print — so he didn't help *these* children at all.

How come it's always the people with defects in logic that get to determine our writing code? Coote didn't want to give us a simplified new spelling system because he didn't want to confuse children. Yet for all intents and purposes he gave these same children that he cared so much about a complicated old system instead! Could it be that deep down inside, this man named Coote knew exactly what he was doing to these kids? Is it possible he meant to annoy them? After all, with a name like *Coote*, it's highly unlikely they missed any opportunity to irritate him first.

COOTE'S SPELLING BOOK   The major purpose of any spelling book is to help children spell better. This first spelling book, however, because of its endorsement of complex spelling, may in the long run have done the opposite.

Silly old Coot!!

THE ENGLISH SCHOOLE-MASTER

Apple Book Camel Dance Dunce

EDMUND COOTE

76

THE INFLUENCE AND INFLUENCES OF EDMUND COOTE

As already indicated, Edmund Coote wasn't the only person involved in the final stabilization of English spelling. Apart from the obvious contributions of the quality printers and the better scribes, a succession of radical reform books, which emerged in the second half of the 16th century, played an important roll. These books called for sweeping spelling reforms based primarily on phonetics. They often rejected traditional and current spelling entirely and wanted to eliminate a great many of our silent and double letters. Some of them even suggested new letters to compensate for the inadequacies of our old ones.

Not surprisingly, these radical reform books — like most that have followed since — achieved little success. They did accomplish two things, though. First, they brought greater awareness to the fact that our system was in turmoil. Second, they annoyed the dickens out of the prominent late 16th-century educator, Richard Mulcaster, prompting him to publish a book that mounted a successful argument against them. The book in question is *The Elimentarie* (1582). As touched upon previously, it is thought (and many similarities suggest) that Edmund Coote was influenced by this publication.

In his book, Richard Mulcaster proposes a stable spelling system based primarily on the accepted customs of the day, with a generous number of changes here and there to regularize things a bit. Edmund Coote also based his system on accepted customs; however, Mr. Coote more closely aligned himself with the commonest spelling in print. This brought him closer to the spelling of the quality printers, which in turn tied him back to the spelling of the better scribes (who are inextricably linked to the clerks of the Royal Chancery from the late Middle-English period). This means that although our spelling was finally stabilized in the 17th century, the meager beginnings of this successful equilibrium began back in the first half of the 15th century. That, without question, is a long time to wait for stability.

During the 17th century there were many other spelling books (in addition to Edmund Coote's *English Schoole-Master*) that aided in the stabilization process. Furthermore, the early English dictionaries — which first came into existence in this century — also played their part in the process. Despite the independent contribution of these publications, however, many of them in one way or another were influenced by the enormously popular *English Schoole-Master*. In fact, the very first English dictionary, *A Table Alphabeticall* (1604), was not only influenced by this document, it copied a great many words directly from its spelling list.[65]

So the first comprehensive spelling book and the first English dictionary (which many of the other 17th-century spelling books and dictionaries evolved from) were, in essence, substantially compiled by Edmund Coote. That makes Mr. Coote a card-carrying member of the English Spelling Hall of Infamy, in my book.

Richard Mulcaster — through his important publication — is also thought to have had considerable influence on the spelling books and dictionaries of the 17th century. His acceptance into the Hall of Infamy is pending, though, since there's a suggestion he may have done our spelling some good. I guess there's a first time for everything.

OUR 350 YEAR OLD SPELLING SYSTEM

Because the greatest part of our spelling system was stabilized by the middle of the 17th century, some among us use this information as an excuse and say things like, "Our spelling system is as bad as it is because it was stabilized 350 years ago." As I've tried my hardest to indicate, though, the fact that our spelling was stabilized 350 years ago in itself has very little to do with the unhealthy state it's in right now. The problem is that,

350 years ago, some of the spelling that was chosen was already 350 years old. Some of it was 750 years old, and some of it (most of it, actually) wasn't even good to begin with. In other words, the spelling that was stabilized in the 17th century was already bad before time added its bit of distortion to it. The truth is, people who were alive in the 17th century often had the same problems with spelling as we have now. Wow! To think that 350 years ago a society existed that had a spelling system just like ours. Frankly, I would have expected more from them.

A SMALL SAMPLE OF THE MANY SPELLINGS THAT WERE ALREADY OLD BEFORE SPELLING STABILIZED IN THE 17TH CENTURY	
LATE 17TH-CENTURY AND MODERN-DAY STABLE SPELLING	MINIMUM AGE OF SPELLING IN THE MIDDLE OF THE 17TH CENTURY
discipline	350 years
violence	360 years
lamb	650 years
dead	650 years
word	761 years

Although I've been aware for quite some time that 17th-century people were exposed to the same spelling problems as we are, that awareness became even more intense a few years back while I was helping my son study for one of his Friday morning spelling tests. It was a relatively difficult test dealing with plurals. Therefore, unlike most of his other school assignments, he was working on this one with me. At least he was for awhile, until he suddenly lay down his pencil and donned his philosophical expression — the one he always dons before asking me questions about subjects I like so he can avoid work. This time, however, that expression almost earned him extra work, because he asked me about a subject I hate — spelling.

"Dad," he said with furrowed brow, "why, when we add *s* to the words *baby* and *lady* do we change the *y's* to *ie's* first, yet last week when we added *ing* to the words *die* and *tie*, we changed the *ie's* to *y's* first?"

He had me stumped there. Now we both had furrowed brows. At the time he asked that question, I wished I had asked it because it was a good one. Still, in retrospect, I'm glad I didn't because while I was searching through the mountain of books hidden in the toilet (where I always excuse myself before answering any of my children's pop quizzes) I found that a similar inquiry had already been made by a man named Richard Hodges back in 1643.[66] Hodges was a schoolmaster and he didn't know the answer to that question, either. Nor did anyone else in any of the other books in my lavatory library. So I returned from the washroom, relieved that it wasn't just me. For 350 years, no one (that I could find, anyway) had been able to solve that puzzle. I then knew for sure that these are centuries-old problems we are having. A lot of good that information was to a curious child searching for a commonsense solution for one of life's many problems, though. Consequently, I told my son what any father in my position would have told him: "Shut up and do your homework; you've got a test in the morning." Then after a while I added, "what did you think of that soccer game last Sunday?" Fathers need breaks too, you know. Especially fathers who have more trouble with the subject at hand than the kids do.

The 17th century was a transitional period. Printers' spelling went from relatively stable, irritating and irrational to extremely stable, irritating, and irrational. These poor 17th-century souls

— just think of the trauma they must have had to go through as they changed from one lousy system to another.[67] Still, as is often said as consolation when something really bad like this happens, at least they had their health. Wait a minute — 17th century. Isn't that the time when tens of thousands died of the plague in England and many more thousands died of disease and hardship in the American colonies? Damn, these 17th-century people had it rough.

Chapter 10
18TH-CENTURY CRYSTALLIZATION (THE CENTURY OF THE DICTIONARY)

The 18th century is the period when English dictionaries came into their own. As stated earlier, English dictionaries actually started in the 17th century with *A Table Alphabeticall* (1604) by Robert Cawdrey. This was followed by several others, including one by the nephew of the poet John Milton, *The New World of English Words* (1658). All these dictionaries were made and published in Britain. The first English dictionary made and published in America didn't make its appearance until 1798. That's 194 years after the first British dictionary and 191 years after the establishment of the first English-American colony.

As chronologically superior as the early British dictionaries are, they were generally limited to scholarly words, or words that seemed scholarly because they were foreign. So they weren't exactly the jam-packed, multi-worded dictionaries we have today. All that changed early in the 18th century when more comprehensive dictionaries, such as John Kersey's *A New English Dictionary* (1702), came onto the scene. These new wordbooks were still pre-pubescent compared to the ones we have now, but as the century progressed they became steadily more and more mature. This maturity culminated in 1755 with a dictionary that was so grown-up that it reigned as the daddy of all English dictionaries for at least 100 years after it was first published. It was written by Samuel Johnson, one of the most renowned literary figures in England at that time.

Some swear by this two-volume wordbook and say it's the best that's ever been written. Others swear *at* it, say it's the worst that's ever been written, and blame Dr. Johnson (as he was later called) for consciously causing every annoying inconsistency in our spelling scheme. What I choose to believe, however, is neither of these two extremes. Johnson's dictionary wasn't the best that's ever been written, because the best that's ever been written has never been written yet. It also wasn't the worst that's ever been written because there were already some doozies out there before Dr. Johnson was even born. Furthermore, Johnson can't possibly be to blame for all our annoying inconsistencies because the greatest part of our spelling was already stable before he laid his big meaty, influential paws upon it.

SOME OF THE THOUSANDS OF WORDS THAT WERE ALREADY STABLE BEFORE JOHNSON INCLUDED THEM IN HIS DICTIONARY				
MODERN-DAY SPELLING	JOHNSON'S 18TH-CENTURY SPELLING	COOTE'S 17TH-CENTURY SPELLING	SOME OF THE PRINTERS' 16TH-CENTURY VARIATIONS	SOME OF THE SCRIBES' MIDDLE-ENGLISH VARIATIONS
slaughter	slaughter	slaughter	slauter, slaughter, slawghter	slawter, slaghter, slaughter
pamphlet	pamphlet	pamphlet	Pamflet, Pamflett, pamphlet	pamflet, pamfilet, paunflet
cease	cease	cease	sese, seas, cease	sese, sees, ceese
broad	broad	broad	brod, brode, broad	brod, brad, brood
build	build	build	bild, bilde, build	bild, bulde, buyld

83

I would love to give an example here of at least one spelling which Johnson personally created that has made our system worse than it would have been without his input. Unfortunately, though, I'm not so sure there are any. All the examples that others have given have proven through the years to be somewhat unreliable. Johnson, for instance, didn't put the *h* in *ghastly* as some have suggested. That particular spelling has been in use since the 16th century. It was used by the printers of Shakespeare, Addison, Dryden, and many other famous writers. Likewise, Johnson wasn't responsible for putting the *g* in *sovereign*. The silent letter in that word has been around since the 1300s.

Dr. Johnson was similarly free of responsibility for inserting the *p* in *receipt* and the *b* in *debt*. He wasn't even the first to record the distinction between the spellings *flower* and *flour*. This, according to the *Oxford English Dictionary* was done in *Cruden's Concordance* in 1738.

Johnson may have favored one variant form over another — for instance, he indicated preferences for *entire* over *intire* and *ache* over *ake* — and this may have affected our spelling slightly. He may also have been a little less eager to pick more recent trends in spelling than other dictionary-makers of his time. In general, however, as reflected in the following quotations, he changed our spelling very little: "Johnson, in fact, merely codified the conventions already adopted by the printers." *Spelling*, page 129; "the truth is", as *A History of English Spelling* says on page 82, "Johnson was powerless to do more than record the already established conventions."

Why, then, if Dr. Johnson didn't make very many changes do I find myself antagonized by this man? And why do I think he's one of the most destructive forces our spelling has ever seen? The answer is simple. I'm antagonized, not by the few changes he may or may not have made, but by the vast number he definitely *didn't* make. Johnson, more than anyone else who went before him in the Modern-English period, had both the intellect and the influence to make things happen for the better — yet he didn't. I can understand Caxton not using his opportunity. He had the power (of the printing press), but not the knowledge of words that Johnson had. I can even understand Coote not simplifying things. Like Johnson, Coote had a great deal of know-how about the subject of spelling, but he didn't have the clout to carry it through. I can't, however, accept any excuse from Johnson. Above all others, he must have been keenly aware of the absurdities in English spelling, because he wrote a book that featured them — his dictionary. He also had the power to do something about it. A demonstration of Johnson's power can be found in his dictionary. In that book he defines a person who writes a dictionary as "a harmless drudge." If he had the authority to get away with lies like that, then I'm sure he could have spelled any way he darned well pleased, and the public would have believed that to be the truth too, and copied him.

A Definition From Samuel Johnson's Dictionary, *A Dictionary of the English Language* (1755)

LEXICOGRAPHER.
A writer of dictionaries; **a harmless drudge**, that busies himself in tracing the original, and detailing the signification of words.

The idea of a dictionary helping to simplify the spelling of a whole country wasn't a new concept in the 18th century. The French were already involved in such a process several years before Dr. Johnson's dictionary came out. In 1740, the French Academy, an institution set up to protect and purify the French language, published the third edition of its historic dictionary, *Dictionnaire de l'Académe Française*. In that issue the academy finally had the courage, after 105 years of existence, to make some worthwhile and necessary improvements to the French spelling system. These changes, coupled with further improvements in the fourth edition of the dictionary in 1762, simplified the spelling of thousands of commonly used French words. This has made the French writing system of today not only easier to spell than it used to be, but easier to read as well.

The French spelling system is still extremely complicated compared to Spanish and Italian, both of which have been more successfully simplified. It is, however, much less complex than the convoluted mass of inconsistencies that pass for a system in our language. French still has too many superfluous silent and double letters, and it still has too many different spellings for single sounds, but it is much more regular and a lot less irritating than English. The French Academy, in conjunction with the various editions of its dictionary, played an important part in this.

There was no *English* Academy in the 18th century, just as there is none now. Therein lies one of the major reasons for the English language's continued failure in the area of spelling. Instead of England setting up an academy and publishing a dictionary like the French did, a group of booksellers commissioned Samuel Johnson to create an authoritative dictionary that would document and control the English language on its own. This set in motion the codifying and legitimizing of the chaotic spelling system we have inherited today.

Johnson was a conservative man who preferred the complexity of accepted custom to the simplicity of personal innovation. He was aware of the innumerable irregularities in our spelling system, but he accepted them as a natural part of life. This is how he put it: "Every language has its anomalies, which, though inconvenient...must be tolerated among the imperfections of human things."[68]

Here are a few of the anomalies that we humans have to tolerate today because of their inclusion in Dr. Johnson's dictionary. He listed *hark* yet *hearken, high* yet *height, rough* yet *ruffian*. He also recorded *four* yet *forty* and *speak* yet *speech*. More generally, he documented *proceed* yet *concede* — and to throw us off completely, *supersede*. He had *fashion, pension, mission, nation, suspicion*, and *complexion*.

One place Johnson was more consistent, though, was in his documentation of words with '*ough*-spellings. He had *dough, bought, through, tough, cough,* and *bough*. Unfortunately, like now, they all had different sounds!

Samuel Johnson did not create any of these spellings. He did, however, legitimize their existence by recording them in a commanding way in his authoritative dictionary. He also recorded, in an equally commanding way, all the foreign words that came to us with foreign spellings from foreign languages over the centuries. Thus, he handed down to posterity words like *rendezvous, silhouette,* and *exhilarate*.

All the ridiculously spelled words I've mentioned, plus thousands more, were given unwarranted respectability by their appearance in Dr. Johnson's dictionary. Is it any wonder my hands go into strangulation mode at the thought of this man? Another reason the mere mention of Johnson's name sends irritated impulses up and down my brain stem is that, before him, we still had a chance for change. Our spelling was only *stable* before he got hold of it, not *crystallized*. It had been in the process of stabilization a number of times before and had always managed to break free. Johnson's authority killed any possibility of that ever happening again. His dictionary locked our spelling in place before the really outrageous combinations had a chance to be simplified, or before the needless complexity of the whole system was brought to the attention of someone who could do something about it. Prior to Johnson there was still a faint glimmer of hope that some enlightened soul would come along and fix what was so obviously broken, but I'm sure the good Doctor's motto was: *If it's broke, leave it alone.*

Ironically, it is widely reported that Johnson did in fact *fix* our spelling. These reports, however, are not referring to *fix* in the repair sense of the word. They are talking about *fix* in the stuck-there-for-good sense. A fixed formation, jammed-in-position-type fixing. Johnson wasn't interested in correcting our spelling problems. All he wanted was for spelling, no matter how bad it was, just to stop changing from generation to generation, to allow people to at least know what the standard is. This is how he himself put it in the preface to his dictionary: "for the law to be known, is of more importance than to be right."[69] Little did this man realize that in future generations many people wouldn't even be able to *read* because of the complicated spelling he immortalized — and, because of that, *all* laws would be unknown to them. So he also *fixed* spelling in another sense of the word, like pet owners do their kitty-cats, without fully considering the users of the service.

THE PERSONALITY OF JOHNSON

To understand the motivations behind Dr. Johnson's choice of spelling, it is essential to appreciate the hardships he endured before writing his dictionary. His first disappointment in life was the development of an infection while still being breast-fed, which left him visually impaired in his right eye and almost blind in his left. In time, he also went deaf in his left ear. Not long after this first infection, he contracted a disease called scrofula. This swelled his neck and face, making him extremely hard to buy pullover sweaters for — prompting his mother to either purchase them too large or knit them right on him. As if these things alone weren't enough to create a serial killer, never mind a spelling fixer, Johnson then contracted smallpox. This converted his big face into a big lumpy face and then into a 3-D map of the moon. To top this all off, he grew to be a giant of a man who twitched and gyrated continuously like he was being given electric shock treatments (which many people thought he should have). This was all gift-wrapped in the most poverty-stricken garb that no money could buy. He was a slob. A poor slob at that.

Johnson's one saving grace was his great intellect. Even a brain as fabulous as his, though, had its problems: he suffered from continuous bouts of absentmindedness, procrastination, and depression. Plus he had his phobias. He feared damnation, which isn't totally unexpected since he was often told he deserved it; he feared insanity, though some said it was far too late for him to worry about that; he also had an extremely strong fear of death, which is surprising, really, because if I had as many things wrong with me as he had, I'd have welcomed it.

It is hardly necessary for me to mention this, but all the things that were wrong with Johnson didn't exactly lead to him becoming a well-adjusted adult. They led to him becoming a man who detested just about everybody and everything he laid his one bad eye on. He seemed to hate everyone who wasn't him — I'm not even sure he wasn't on the list. Even the things he liked, he didn't like as much as other people. Here is what he said about music: "of all the noises, I think music is the least disagreeable."[70] Remind me never to use this man as a reference on a résumé.

Over and above the everyday variety of hatred, Johnson seemed to have a special elevated repulsion for people who weren't English. Americans, for instance, he wasn't too fond of. He called them "a race of convicts."[71] He wasn't too keen on Scotsmen either, which is peculiar because he surrounded himself with them. His biographer and close associate, James Boswell, was a Scotsman. Five of the six assistants who helped him write his dictionary were of the kilted variety. At face value, this seems contradictory, but in the preface to his dictionary he wrote that he had written it with "little assistance of the learned."[72] So it's obvious the only reason he liked having Scotsmen around was to tick them off later by writing things like that. Now we know where his fear of death came from.

Johnson didn't just hate with words, though. On occasions, he made a real spectacle of himself by punching people out who *really* rubbed him the wrong way. A harmless drudge indeed. One of the people he got physical with was a bookseller. So given the fact that it was a group of booksellers who commissioned him to write his dictionary, the blame for the spelling in that dictionary must land squarely on Johnson's shoulders because after that first demonstration of annoyance, I can't imagine any bookseller ever going against anything he ever did or said again. "No, no, Sam. The dictionary is perfect. I'd have settled for simpler spelling, but hey, I like it the way you did it. Nice suit by the way. Burlap, isn't it?" Who can blame them for groveling. In the 18th century, even monsters used to check under their beds at night to make sure Dr. Johnson wasn't hiding there.

Without question, Johnson was all the things I said he was. Through all his anger and aggression, though, there was still a hint of a more civilized person lurking beneath the surface. This was the side of him that led people to say he could be kind and generous, but it's the side of him that I put down to absentmindedness. He just forgot who he really was for a moment, which was a cantankerous old so-and-so whose terrorization was so great that it has now become a sign of stupidity not to spell his stupid way.

THE ALTERNATIVE TO JOHNSON

Tell me honestly now, with an unbiased objective opinion of this man (bearing in mind that my description of him is steeped in truth): is Johnson the kind of individual you might expect would want to make things easy for other people? Would he be your preference for a candidate to finally fix our spelling so we could understand our laws better? Does he strike you as the type of person interested in helping us to read better, when he needed a magnifying glass and a seeing-eye ant to find his own place? He certainly wouldn't be my first pick. I'd have impartially chosen one of the Scotsmen. Any one of them would do; spin a bottle. You can be sure a Scotsman would keep words as short and simple as possible, because every second spent on unimportant things like spelling means less time spent in the pub. Put a Scotsman in charge of our spelling and we'd have ended the 18th century not with Johnson's two big volumes, but with a dictionary whose words were so short that even the paperback edition would need hard covers to stop it from blowing away in the wind.

DICTIONARIES AND SPELLING IN
18TH-CENTURY AMERICA

As established, the first dictionary written and published in America did not appear until the end of the 18th century. Because of this, British dictionaries — especially Johnson's — had a dominant affect on 18th-century American spelling. In his book, *The American Language*, H.L. Mencken says this about Johnson and the spelling within his dictionary: "His influence was tremendous, both in England and in America."[73]

When Johnson's dictionary came out in 1755, America was still following the British lead regarding the proper etiquette of spelling.[74] American spelling was still slightly behind the British model; however, faster transportation, better distribution networks, and an ever-improving standard of living and education were closing the gap considerably.

Being physically separate from Britain, the American colonies obviously developed *some* of their own spelling tendencies in the 18th century. These tendencies, among other things, included spelling words such as *honor, color* and *favor* quite frequently with an *or* rather than an *our*.[75] Despite the seemingly homegrown influences, though, America was still being bombarded with British models to emulate. The majority of books sold in America, for instance, were still imported from England, textbooks were traditionally published in London, and British dictionaries were commonplace. American publishers being influenced by their British counterparts didn't help matters, either.

Even during the revolutionary war years in the latter half of the century, when Britain — to say the least — was out of favor with American colonists, British spelling ruled supreme. Even the Declaration of Independence — the highest level of revolutionary documentation — was printed (for all practical purposes) using British spelling.[76] Exactly 300 years (minus five months) after Caxton first printed in England, the first printed public document of the United States of America was still affected by Caxton's and other British people's horrible choices of spelling.

The First Few Sentences From The First Printing Of
The Declaration of Independence (1776)[77]
(Apart from the two underlined words, the spelling in this
example was and is correct for both the United States and Britain)

In CONGRESS, July 4, 1776.
A DECLARATION
By the REPRESENTATIVES of the
UNITED STATES OF AMERICA,
In GENERAL CONGRESS assembled.

When in the Course of human Events, it becomes necessary for one People to dissolve the Political Bands which have connected them with another, and to assume among the Powers of the Earth, the separate and equal Station to which the Laws of Nature and of Nature's God entitle them, a decent Respect to the Opinions of Mankind requires that they should declare the causes which impel them to the separation.

We hold these Truths to be self-evident, that all Men are created equal, that they are endowed by their Creator with certain unalienable Rights, that among these are Life, Liberty, and the Pursuit of Happiness— That to secure these Rights, Governments are instituted among Men, deriving their just Powers from the Consent of the Governed, that whenever any Form of Government becomes destructive of these Ends, it is the Right of the People to alter or to abolish it, and to institute new Government, laying its Foundation on such Principles, and organizing its Powers in such Form, as to them shall seem most likely to effect their Safety and Happiness. Prudence, indeed, will dictate that Governments long established should not be changed for light and transient Causes; and accordingly all Experience <u>hath shewn</u>, that Mankind are most disposed to suffer, while Evils are sufferable, than to right themselves by abolishing the Forms to which they are accustomed.

A few cunning colonists attempted to take advantage of the anti-British sentiment during and immediately after the revolution by pushing their simplified spelling agenda. These people obviously didn't understand the attachment English speakers have to their spelling system. As bad as it was and as much as the colonists wanted to split from the country that created it, they still wanted to keep British spelling.

In the late 18th century, even the American accent was starting to change from the British accent, yet still Americans kept the spelling of Britain.[78] As the famous song almost said, "You say *tomayto* and I say *tomahto*, but we both spell it the same way."

It seems to me that during the revolution the prospect of changing to another language was given more consideration than the prospect of changing to a new system of spelling. In the heat of rhetorical and physical battle, some radical patriots are said to have proposed that the language spoken in America should change to French. Others apparently suggested Hebrew or Greek. Since 90 percent of the people in the 13 colonies descended from English-speaking people, though, these proposals did not progress too far.

It has also been reported that German was considered for a while as the official American language.[79] This proposal no doubt firmed up people's allegiance to the *English* language, even with its horrible spelling. It seems the American people wanted political independence, but very few wanted to change the way they spelled. As David Simpson says in *The Politics of American English, 1776–1850* (1986), page 33: "it was to prove more difficult to declare independence from Samuel Johnson than it had been to reject George III."

The first significant and probably most important character to attempt to change American spelling from the British model was the great American inventor and statesman, Benjamin Franklin. In-between flying his kite in the rain and telling people that a "penny saved is a penny earned," he worked on a new alphabet and spelling system that, if ever fully developed, I'm sure would have been as practical as the bifocals he invented or as warm and cozy as his stove.

Franklin was an important and powerful American leader. He was a journalist, a philosopher, an ambassador extraordinaire. As one of the Founding Fathers of the U.S., he not only signed, but also helped frame, both the Declaration of Independence and the U.S. Constitution. He was (and did) all these things, yet he was unable to influence the American public and their printers sufficiently enough for them to simplify their spelling.

Other would-be American spelling reformers were William Thornton and James Ewing. The most important, though, because he did bring about some change, was the great American lexicographer, Noah Webster. Webster started his reform activism in the wake of the revolution, but was unable to achieve much change until the century that followed. Since Webster's impact and influence on American spelling did not occur until the 19th century, that is where it's discussed in detail. It is sufficient to say here that Webster changed American spelling a lot less than people generally think. American spelling was a few years behind British spelling prior to Webster. His meager reforms, however, only catapulted America spelling to a fraction of a nanosecond in front.

Webster became an American lexicographer of great distinction. Before him, though, there were other individuals involved with dictionaries in America who deserve a mention. The first dictionary printed but not written in America was the *Royal Standard English Dictionary* authored by William Perry. This work was published in Massachusetts in 1788. It was a popular and important dictionary in the U.S.

The first dictionary written as well as published in America was entitled *A School Dictionary*. It was printed only two years before the end of the century in 1798. This dictionary probably had no direct influence on American spelling — or much else for that matter — since by all accounts it wasn't a greatly original work. The author readily admits his material was collected from "previous authors of established reputation." These previous authors are thought to be William Perry and Dr. Samuel Johnson.[80]

Despite its unoriginality, there is one very important historic feature about this dictionary that should be noted — it was written by Samuel Johnson Junior. His famous father must have been so proud. His famous father being Samuel Johnson, first president of King's College, the current Columbia University, not Dr. Samuel Johnson who thankfully had no children.

Chapter 11
19TH-CENTURY AMERICANIZATION (THE CENTURY OF AMERICAN REFORM)

When I stated earlier that the spelling of the 18th century (and beyond) wasn't much different from our own, that didn't mean there haven't been any changes since then. It merely meant the changes that have occurred haven't in any great way improved or impaired the overall state of our spelling. In other words, the changes have been relatively insignificant. Having established that piece of earth-shattering information, we now focus our attention, for the bulk of the 19th century, almost completely on the spelling of the United States of America. We do this because the most significant of these insignificant changes happened in the United States. Beyond that, though, we do it because concentrating on Britain would bore us to snores, since nothing much happened in Britain at this time — apart from the negative reactions to what was happening in America.

In the United States in the year 1807, Noah Webster (writer, lecturer, schoolmaster, former lawyer, former judge, former child) started working on a project that would eventually manifest itself in 1828 as the greatest English dictionary the world had ever known to that date. This landmark publication is so important in the history of English dictionaries that now, in the U.S., the word *Webster* means dictionary — as everyone called Webster is no doubt aware. (Even as small children, people called Webster think they're being teased when their parents point to broken toys and say "Webster, what's the meaning of this?")

This dictionary, apart from all its other qualities (nice cover, superior binding, weights and measures chart on the back) was a major player in the establishment of reformed spelling in America. Now, *reformed spelling* is one of those terms that mean one thing in Britain and another thing in the United States, therefore, before I continue, I'll define it in both languages. For Americans, reformed spelling simply means "spelling that has been altered to make it easier." For the British, who have never really had it, it more elaborately means "a highly imaginative, hypothetical situation in which someone actually has the audacity to alter the letters in words to make these words better, but in the process making them no longer British."

Americans have to remember that Britain is steeped in tradition. Up to its eyeballs in the stuff, actually. That's why even though Webster's spelling was well received in the United States, its acceptance in Britain was largely limited to being respectfully dubbed, *American spelling*. Or alternatively, *Yankee gobshite!* — and it doesn't take a degree in British phraseology to figure out what that means.

A FEW OF THE SPELLINGS CHOSEN BY WEBSTER IN HIS 1828 DICTIONARY THAT HAVE BEEN RESPECTFULLY DUBBED *AMERICAN*			
MODERN-DAY AMERICAN SPELLING	WEBSTER'S PREFERRED SPELLING (1828)	JOHNSON'S PREFERRED SPELLING (1755)	MODERN-DAY BRITISH SPELLING
ax	ax	axe	axe
plow	plow	plough	plough
color	color	colour	colour
woolen	woolen	woollen	woollen
vise (clamp)	vise	vice	vice

So Webster did well to alter the American portion of a tradition of non-simplification that had lasted for over 1200 years to this point. He did what many distinguished scholars and well-respected individuals had tried to do since the Renaissance: simplify English spelling. He succeeded where others for the most part were totally unsuccessful. In fact, just as the word *Webster* is now synonymous with *dictionary,* before Webster the word *reform* was synonymous with *failure.*

Webster's dictionary helped change all that, but it wasn't the lone player in the breaking of this trend. It is thought that yet another spelling book, *The American Spelling Book*, played an even greater part in the establishment of reformed spelling in the U.S.A. A well-known encyclopedia had this to say about *The American Spelling Book*: "it did much to settle and standardize American spelling."[81] Other publications show much less restraint when they commit to paper such unbridled statements as, "*The American Spelling Book* had much more influence on American spelling than Webster's dictionary did." That last comment may surprise and even annoy some people (especially the person I was paraphrasing), but I'm sure Webster wouldn't have raised an eyebrow or lowered a lip at what it says because it is essentially a compliment to him. You see, the writer of the dictionary and the writer of the spelling book were one and the same person: Noah Webster. It seems to me what we could have here is a lowdown, despicably sneaky, double-barreled way for a spelling reformer to get his spelling accepted. Why don't we try that again sometime?

If we do try that kind of trickery again, though, we should make a concerted effort on this occasion to achieve something worthwhile. Because with all due respect, I don't consider American spelling to *be* worthwhile. I think it's a step up from British spelling, but then so is hieroglyphics. The truth is, American spelling is not much different than its British counterpart, so it was hardly worth the effort to change it.

Once again, I'm sure a portion of the population will question my judgment here, because people have been led to believe the differences between American and British spellings are much greater than they actually are. This is a common misconception and Professor John W. Clark in the book *Spelling* explains why: "Though the differences [between American and British spellings] are not of many kinds, three or four of them appear in very considerable numbers of quite common words."[82]

One of the differences the good professor was talking about is the *or/our* difference — i.e., in the U.S., *honor*, *humor*, and *flavor* are the established spellings, whereas in Britain these same words are spelled *honour, humour,* and *flavour*. These examples are only one *kind* of difference. That one kind, though — plus a small number of others — affects a great many words and helps make American spelling appear a lot better than it actually is. Now all we have to do is make American spelling easier to spell than it actually is. Then we'll really have a winner.

SOME OF THE VERY FEW *KINDS* OF DIFFERENCES BETWEEN AMERICAN AND BRITISH SPELLING		
KIND OF DIFFERENCE	AMERICAN SPELLING	BRITISH SPELLING
or/our	labor	labour
	behavior	behaviour
	neighbor	neighbour
er/re	center	centre
	luster	lustre
	somber	sombre
se/ce	offense	offence
	defense	defence
	pretense	pretence
ol/oul	molt	moult
	mold	mould
	smolder	smoulder
l/ll	traveler	traveller
	leveler	leveller
	shoveler	shoveller

Anyone who still doesn't believe that American spelling is much more difficult than it need be should ask the following question: How come the United States has had, and still has, some of the hardest-working and most determined simplified spelling organizations ever assembled on this planet?[83] Is it because these organizations think American spelling is perfect? I don't think so. It's because they know American spelling still has a long way to go before it's even as good as people think it is already. How far it still has to go is epitomized in the complex spelling of the word *neighbor*. In Britain, that word is spelled *neighbour*. Webster's influence changed the *our* to *or*. Now I ask you, if you were an alien from outer space who came down to earth and looked at that word before Webster's influence altered it, would you have changed the *our* to *or* first? Would you have stayed to talk to someone who did? No wonder we only catch glimpses of these alien beings before they dart off into the distance disguised as giant silver cigars. I wouldn't want to talk to a civilization that thought this was significant progress either. I'd get the dickens out of there and fast, before I caught whatever it was they had.

THE ALTERNATIVES FROM WEBSTER

Despite the obvious limitations, I would have been quite content with Webster's reforms if it weren't for the fact that this man, who gave us so little, at one time wanted to give us so much more. That's right. Thirty-nine years before he brought out his dictionary, Webster published a book called *Dissertations on the English Language*. In that book he called for the type of simplified spelling that gives would-be reformers semi-moist dreams. Seductive spellings like *laf* and *bilt* and *tung* filled its pages. These spellings looked peculiar even then, but if Webster had stuck to that 1789 book (like he should have) they would look as perfect as a princess to us now. Which would help explain why some would-be reformers have wet dreams about them.

For all its faults, American spelling is lucky to have progressed even as far as it did, because that wasn't the first time Webster had changed his mind. Only six years before that radical reform book came out, he published his first book, *A Grammatical Institute of the English Language*, and the spelling recommended in that book was copied straight from the dictionary of Johnson. It was also dead against reformed spelling. This I find surprising, because that first book of Webster's was actually an early version of his *American Spelling Book* — the spelling book which, if you remember, was greatly responsible for establishing reformed spelling in the U.S.

What a mind-changer Webster was. He reversed his decisions more times than a politician on a polygraph machine. He's a great person to quote in an argument, though, because no matter what side you're on, at one time or another he's been passionately for (or against) that position, too.

SOME OF WEBSTER'S MIND-CHANGING BOOKS AND THE RECOMMENDED SPELLING WITHIN THEM		
BOOK TITLE	RECOMMENDED SPELLING	DATE OF PUBLICATION
A Grammatical Institute of the English Language, Part 1 *	Johnson-type Spelling (British Spelling)	1783
Dissertations on the English Language	Radical Reformed Spelling (Simplified Spelling)	1789
An American Dictionary of the English Language	Conservative Reformed Spelling (American Spelling)	1828

* This book is an early version of *The American Spelling Book*. The title changed in later editions; likewise the spelling.

THE PERSONALITY OF WEBSTER

At first-, second- and third-hundredth glance, Webster seems to have been a complete yo-yo, going from one extreme to another and then most of the way back again. However, after a thorough examination of his writings, coupled with my extensive knowledge of little-known medical disorders, I have determined that Webster was not exhibiting any of the symptoms normally associated with the dysfunction *yo-yo* — i.e., head-spinning, strung-out feeling, etc. What he was suffering from, though, was a multiple personality disorder called *Sybil-osis*, caused by having too many current and former professions. The teacher in him brought out the first book with the Johnsonian spelling in it, because teaching and checking difficult spelling is a large part of what teachers do. Later, the writer in him brought out the radical reform book because the elimination of elements not essential to the writing process is the goal of all good writers. After that, when his 1828 dictionary was being worked on, the lawyer in him manifested itself, causing words to get long and complicated again, almost canceling out all the good work of the writer.

Don't think the changes stopped there all the same, because they didn't. When the second edition of his dictionary came out two years before he died, even fewer of the reforms that survived in the first edition survived in the second one. I think what we were seeing there was the former child in him. It is said that people revert to being children as they get older. Webster was 83 then. People of that age often have very, very young minds.

Although in the end I am ultimately happy that Webster was able to live to a ripe old age, I must admit I am extremely thankful he dropped dead when he did because the way things were going, given a few more years and he'd have been right back where he started with Johnsonian spelling. Furthermore, a few more years after that, and he'd have developed a system that would make Johnson's spelling look like radical reform. Then the British would have loved it. It would appeal to their sense of pomposity. They'd have called it, respectfully, English.

This has been a confusing century, with Webster's views flip-flopping like live fish in a frying pan, so I've decided to go against respected literary convention here and sum it up: Webster the teacher, *minus* Webster the writer, *plus* Webster the lawyer, *plus* Webster the child *equals* not much better than Johnson — tip and tax included.

This chapter on Webster would be incomplete if it failed to reveal he was pulled by one other influential force in his life: the force of Ben Franklin. When Webster performed his first flip-flop from Johnson-type spelling to radical reform, that was Franklin's influence.[84] Unfortunately, as we now know, Webster was soon off the Franklin kick and back on the Johnson fad — from which he sold a stack of books and influenced generations of people.

Thanks to Franklin, Webster came to appreciate the need for spelling reform. In the end, however, like most dictionary-makers, Webster was unable to venture far from what people were used to. Therefore, in reality, Webster, the commonly accepted father of American spelling, was actually the influential stepparent of the continuation of mostly British-type spelling in America.[85] A sad result for such promising earlier potential.

Chapter 12
20TH-CENTURY BRITISHIZATION (THE CENTURY OF BRITISH NON-REFORM)

At the end of the 20th century and the start of the 21st, we now have two extremely stable, firmly fixed, well-and-truly entrenched English spelling customs: one American and one British.[86] And as my Grandpa Angus used to say, "If any one of them was any better they'd still both be rotten." I'm quoting Grandpa out of context, of course. What he was actually referring to was the way my brother and I played soccer. Which only makes that quote even more appropriate here because a better analogy to describe the uncoordinated klutziness of these two spelling systems could never be found, even by viewing old Laurel and Hardy films.

As similarly useless as these two spelling systems are, and as bad as the American system is, I still find myself questioning, as I'm sure many Americans do, why Britain hasn't made a complete changeover to American spelling yet. After all, surely a little improvement is better than no improvement at all. The sad truth is, however, that even though American spelling has been looked upon favorably in Britain by a few advanced thinkers (who were later horsewhipped into reconsidering their positions), and even though there is already some American influence within British spelling, that influence could never be described as a serious contender.[87] There just aren't the makings of a fair fight here. American spelling has to compete against a system that's been in place in Britain for many centuries. To oust a tradition that's already in place in Britain, even if it was only established last Tuesday, would require the oratory genius and motivational skills of a Churchill, not the treasonous remarks of a few advanced thinkers who buckle under at the first sign of a riding crop. Britain has as much chance of making a complete change from British to American spelling as it has of changing its national sport from soccer to American football. And a sport where there isn't a significant chance of spectators being injured just doesn't appeal to the British, even if their grandchildren are absolutely brilliant at it.

The amount of American influence on British spelling at the moment is hard to quantify since many of the so-called American spellings that have risen to the forefront in Britain have been used in Britain for many centuries. For instance, the British use of the following spellings (either as their main choice or as a strong variant) could have more to do with Johnson choosing them in his 1755 dictionary than with Webster choosing them in his 1828 dictionary: *honorary, humorist, organize, pulverize, judgment, deflection, encyclopedia, hemorrhage*, and *wagon*. Johnson spelled these words the U.S.A. way, years before there was a U.S.A!

Tradition in Britain is extremely important. Still, even without the commanding presence of time-honored rituals, any time after the early 20th century was and is the worst time ever to challenge the British spelling system because that's when the ultra-authoritative *Oxford English Dictionary* came out.[88] And to a great extent, that immensely influential document used as its main choice of spelling the British spelling of the day.[89]

The British spelling of the day, incidentally, was for the most part the same as the spelling of the previous 80,000 days. Little had changed since the end of the 17th century, as I predicted back when I was writing about it. Coote's spelling book helped stabilize British spelling in the 17th century, Johnson's dictionary crystallized it after that, and now *The Oxford English Dictionary* paralyzed it.[90] The basic core of British spelling couldn't move now even if the public, the printers, and the Pope wanted it to. Although I doubt very much the Pope would want it changed. He has a vested interest in keeping spelling exactly as it is now because it allows him, even when he's writing in English, to keep up on his Latin.

A FEW OF THE MULTITUDE OF SPELLINGS FOUND IN THE 1928 *OXFORD ENGLISH DICTIONARY* THAT REINFORCED AGE-OLD BRITISH TRADITION				
MODERN-DAY BRITISH SPELLING	OED'S 1928 SPELLING	JOHNSON'S 1755 SPELLING	WEBSTER'S 1828 SPELLING	MODERN-DAY AMERICAN SPELLING
diarrhoea	diarrhoea	diarrhoea	diarrhea	diarrhea
endeavour	endeavour	endeavour	endeavor	endeavor
moulding	moulding	moulding	molding	molding
libellous	libellous	libellous	libelous	libelous
skilful	skilful	skilful	skillful	skillful

THE AUTHORITY OF THE OXFORD ENGLISH DICTIONARY

The 1928 *Oxford English Dictionary* (then known as *A New English Dictionary on Historical Principles*) was a formidable manuscript. How could any meager challenger every hope to overthrow it? It was the unofficial bible of British spelling, which is another reason why the Pope would want to keep it. It held between its covers the history of almost every word commonly used in Britain since writing picked up after the Normans invaded. It also gave all the meanings, grammatical forms, and uses that these words went through, plus many of the spellings. Therefore, it wasn't just the last word in spelling; it was, and is, considered by many to be the "greatest scholarly achievement of all time."

110

A Couple Of Sentences From Page xiv Of
Oxford American Dictionary (1980)

> No dictionary in any language has approached [*The Oxford English Dictionary*] in thoroughness, authority, and wealth of linguistic information. It was considered by many to be **the greatest scholarly achievement of all time** — and still is.

The arrival, formidability, and choice of spelling of the 1928 *Oxford English Dictionary* means that another perfect opportunity to change while riding on the back of great authority has been wasted. The same dictionary that paralyzed British spelling could equally have used its power to make significant strides towards simplicity. It showed many of the spellings each word had gone through, anyway. Surely one more spelling for each word wouldn't have made that much difference. Especially if the new spellings were as short and simple as they should be.

Admittedly, the 1928 *Oxford English Dictionary* did make some changes away from the accepted norm. Some of these changes, such as its preferences for *jail* and *program* over *gaol* and *programme*, even lean towards simplicity. Some even look suspiciously American.[91] Unfortunately, these excursions into the realm of sanity were a rarity.

Many authors claim that the changes made by dictionaries seldom make a difference to the spelling in our everyday lives; nevertheless, if any dictionary could have made *significant* strides towards simplicity and gotten away with it, the 1928 *Oxford English Dictionary* may well have been the one.[92]

Regrettably, these dreams of large-scale simplification didn't come true, and this time the person who missed that great opportunity, I'm sad to say, was a Scotsman. James Augustus Henry Murray of Roxburshire, Scotland, was the chief editor of

111

The Oxford English Dictionary from 1879 to 1915. Although Murray wasn't alive to see this dictionary completed, his organizational skills and the momentum he created are credited with guiding the project through to its conclusion. Wouldn't Johnson be ticked off to discover that a Scotsman edited the dictionary that knocked his out of the number one position in Britain?[93] I'm sure Johnson would be turning in his grave right now at the thought of this; if it weren't for the fact they nailed *him* down instead of the coffin lid to make sure he didn't pop up and bop one of the undertakers.

It may be hard to believe this, but the authority of *The Oxford English Dictionary* didn't come about just because a Scotsman edited it. Nor did it emerge from thin air on account of being "the greatest scholarly achievement of all time." These two things no doubt had an influence on it. The real reason for its authority, however, was quite simply because it was big. And big things (like big people) have a certain do-as-I-say-or-I'll-punch-the-snot-out-of-you look about them.

To fully comprehend how enormous this dictionary is, consider this: Johnson's dictionary was published in 1755, Webster's was published in 1828, while *The Oxford English Dictionary* was published in stages from 1884 to 1928. It took that long, plus 27 more years prior to the first publication date, to put that dictionary's 10 sizable volumes together. Furthermore, currently *The Oxford English Dictionary* has 20 volumes, and each of these is as large as the original ones were. If you're looking for a dictionary for quick reference, nine out of ten people in the know wouldn't pick this one. However, if you're looking for something that can hold a door shut while you escape out a window during a police raid, then this is the set of authoritative books for you.

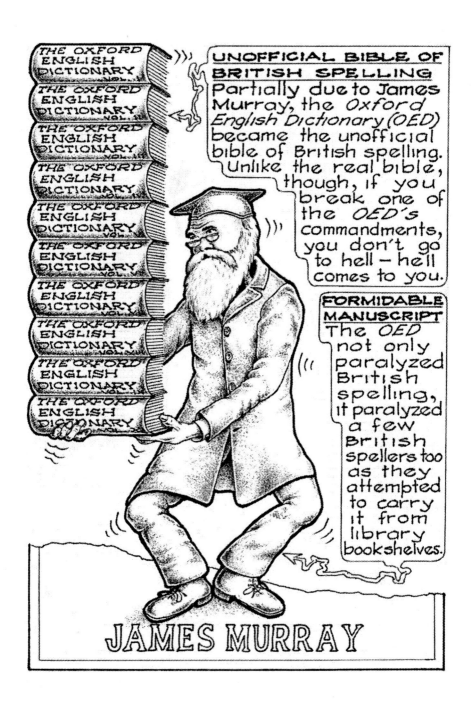

UNOFFICIAL BIBLE OF BRITISH SPELLING

Partially due to James Murray, the *Oxford English Dictionary (OED)* became the unofficial bible of British spelling. Unlike the real bible, though, if you break one of the *OED's* commandments, you don't go to hell — hell comes to you.

FORMIDABLE MANUSCRIPT

The *OED* not only paralyzed British spelling, it paralyzed a few British spellers too as they attempted to carry it from library bookshelves.

JAMES MURRAY

THE PRIDE OF THE BRITISH

It is obvious to me that the purpose of *The Oxford English Dictionary* was never to paralyze British spelling. Its purpose, I'm equally aware, was not the suppression of American spelling. In the final analysis, though, whether the suppression of American spelling was its intent or not is academic, because even without *The Oxford English Dictionary*, the British people would never have adopted, and will never adopt, the overall spelling of America. They're just too proud a nation ever to allow that to happen. As already specified, there is a little bit of American simplification in British spelling at the moment, but it's only in a few weak-willed words that probably would have been equally receptive to American *complication* if Noah Webster had lived long enough to bring that about.

What the proud British have accepted with relative ease, though, is an abundance of uniquely American words and phrases. These different ways of saying things, however, have sneaked into the British psyche via American films, TV programs, and the menus of recently established McDonald's restaurants, so the British aren't really aware of where they came from. If Britain adopts across-the-board American spelling, though, there could be no doubt where that came from. And I can imagine what the loyal British would think about that: "First the conversion of our vocabulary to American," they would say, "then the conversion of our spelling. What next, the conversion of our whole bleedin' language? Soon we'll be led to believe the English tongue started, not when the Anglo-Saxons landed, but when Columbus did!"

No, the British will never completely change to American spelling. I'm as sure of that as I am of death and baldness (hopefully in that order). It's bad enough being out-numbered, out-technologized, and out-gunned by one of their former possessions. To be out-spelled by them too would be the last straw. Spelling is Britain's last bastion of imperialism. Keeping the same spelling that they had when they were once the all-powerful, ever-expanding British Empire is their only defense against being considered a satellite state of America.

These feelings that the British people have about American spelling (in specific) and to a much lesser degree about the American language (in general) were summed up in a not-so-original statement made to me recently by an upper-class English gentleman: "My dear chappie," he said as he twisted and waxed his mustache into the shape of a set of handlebars, "American English is a foreign language and, therefore, should be treated as such."[94]

Surprisingly enough, I agree with him. So why then doesn't Britain wholeheartedly adopt American spelling, like it did with the spelling of every other foreign language that invaded it? At least that way, the English-speaking people of this earth would be saved the embarrassment they have at the moment, of having the two worst alphabetic spelling systems in the entire world. Instead, they'd only have the *one* worst. Now there's something to look forward to. A real suicide discourager if ever I've heard one. I'll remove the dumb-dumb bullets from my gun and wait.

That's where things stand at the moment. I'm waiting patiently while our two stable, but mentally unbalanced, spelling systems become further entrenched by tradition. Still, as compensation, even though these well-entrenched spelling systems live on, the men who helped establish them are all dead now. Not only dead, but eaten by worms, decomposed by maggots and microbes, and possibly even halved in two by a construction backhoe. So, as you can see, the history of English spelling isn't all bad news after all. Oh, I do so love happy endings.

SELECTED BIBLIOGRAPHY

Barnett, Lincoln. *The Treasure of Our Tongue*. New York: Alfred A. Knopf, 1964.

Baugh, Albert C., and Thomas Cable. *A History of the English Language*. New Jersey: Prentice Hall, 1993.

Bede. *A History of the English Church and People*. Translated by Leo Sherley-Price. Revised by R.E. Latham. Harmondsworth, England: Penguin Books Ltd., 1968.

Berlitz, Charles. *Native Tongues*. New York, New York: The Putnam Publishing Group, 1984.

Blake, Norman. *Caxton and his World*. London: Andre Deatsch Ltd., 1968.

Bryson, Bill. *The Mother Tongue, English and how it got that way*. New York, New York: William Morrow and Company, Inc., 1990.

Burchfield, Robert. *The English Language*. Oxford: Oxford University Press, 1985.

Coote, Edmund. *The English Schoole-Maister* (1596). Facsimile. Menston, England: The Scolar Press Ltd., 1968.

Crystal, David. *The Cambridge Encyclopedia of Language*. Cambridge: Cambridge University Press, 1987.

Crystal, David. *The Cambridge Encyclopedia of the English Language*. Cambridge: Cambridge University Press, 1995.

Crystal, David. *The English Language*. London, England: Penguin Books Ltd., 1988.

Fisher, John H., Malcolm Richardson, and Jane L. Fisher. *An Anthology of Chancery English*. Knoxville, Tennessee: The University of Tennessee Press, 1984.

Grambs, David. *Death by Spelling*. New York: Perennial Library, 1989.

Follick, Mont. *The Case for Spelling Reform*. London: Sir Isaac Pitman and Sons Ltd, 1964.

Hart, John. *An Orthographie* (1569). Facsimile. Menston, England: The Scolar Press Ltd., 1969.

Hogg, Richard M. (general editor) *The Cambridge History of the English Language*. Cambridge: Cambridge University Press, 1992 (vols. 1 & 2), 1999 (vol. 3).

Johnson, Samuel. *A Dictionary of the English Language* (1755). Facsimile. New York: AMS Press, Inc., 1967.

Laird, Charlton. *The Miracle of Language*. New York: World Publishing Company, 1953.

McArthur, Tom. *The Oxford Companion to the English Language*. Oxford: Oxford University Press, 1992.

McCrum, Robert, William Cran and Robert MacNeil. *The Story of English*. New York, New York: Elisabeth Sifton Books/Viking, 1986.

Mulcaster, Richard. *The First Part of the Elementary* (1582). Facsimile. Menston, England: The Scolar Press Ltd., 1970.

Murray, K.M. Elisabeth. *Caught in the Web of Words*. New Haven: Yale University Press, 1977.

Noory, Samuel. *Dictionary of Pronunciation*. New York: A.S. Barnes and Co., Inc., 1965.

Pei, Mario. *The Story of the English Language*. Philadelphia & New York: J. B. Lippincott Company, 1967.

Peters, Robert A. *A Linguistic History of English*. Boston: Houghton Mifflin Company, 1968.

Potter, Simeon. *Our Language*. London: Penguin Books, 1976.

Pyles, Thomas. *Words and Ways of American English*. New York: Random House, 1952.

Rondthaler, Edward and Edward J. Lias. *Dictionary of Simplified American Spelling*. New York: The American Language Academy, 1986.

Scragg, D.G. *A History of English Spelling*. Manchester: Manchester University Press, 1974.

Sharp, Stanley L. *The REAL Reason Why Johnny Still Can't Read*. Smithtown, New York: Exposition Press, Inc., 1982.

Vallins, G.H. *Spelling*. Revised by D.G. Scragg. Kent: Tonbridge Printers Limited, 1973.

INDEX

ENDNOTES

1 [From page xiii] Here is what some knowledgeable experts have said about English spelling:

- Dr. John Nist, *A Structural History of English* (1966), page 16: "The spelling practices of modern English are the worst of any major language in the world."
- Dr. Charlton G. Laird, *The Miracle of Language* (1953), page 228: "We have the most erratic spelling of any of the great languages."
- Dr. Mont Follick, *The Case for Spelling Reform* (1965), page 220: "...the biggest spelling-chaos that it has ever been the misfortune of any nation to cope with."
- Dr. Abraham F. Citron, BEtSS (Better Education thru Simplified Spelling) fact sheet, page 3: "...by far the worst and most irrational and inconsistent alphabetic spelling system in the world."
- Dr. Edward Rondthaler and Dr. Edward J. Lias, *Dictionary of Simplified American Spelling* (1986), page 3: "English is by far the most erratically spelled of modern languages."
- Dr. Mario Pei, *The Story of the English Language* (1967), page 338: "The fact remains that our spelling is more than irrational — it is inhuman, and forms the bane not merely of foreigners, but of our own younger generations, compelled to devote interminable hours to learning a system which is the soul and essence of anarchy."

2 [From page xiii] Dr. Sharp's 50-million quotation comes from page 134 of *The REAL Reason Why Johnny Still Can't Read* (1982). Educational Sociologist, Dr.

Abraham F. Citron, wrote this in a letter to me in 1988: "a working estimate of poor or 'bad spellers' in this country at the present time is fifty percent of the adult population." That would give us many millions more than 50 million.

3   [From page xiv] Refer to *Dictionary Of Simplified American Spelling* (1986), page 5, note 2, for a passage about bright children having trouble with our spelling system. Also read *The Story of the English Language* (1967), Page 347, and *The Cambridge Encyclopedia of the English Language* (1987), page 213, for similar information.

4   [From page xiv]. For passages about other languages not needing to teach spelling and not needing spelling books refer to the following publications: *Dictionary Of Simplified American Spelling* (1986), page 5, note 3: "only in English-speaking schools is it necessary to teach spelling." *Detroit Free Press* (Aug. 16, 1981), page 17, article by Suzanne Dolezal: "Spanish kids never see a spelling book in school because they don't need one. Neither do Swedish, Danish or German kids." *Spelling Reform Proposal For The English Language* (1981), a Wayne State University doctoral dissertation by E.V. Starrett: "Children in lands which have fairly phonemic spelling, such as Germany, Denmark, Italy, Spain, and Sweden never see a spelling book." *The Case for Spelling Reform* (1964), page 262: "I have never seen a spelling book in Spain [or] Germany." For other passages on the simplicity and ease of learning the spelling of other languages, read *The REAL Reason Why Johnny Still Can't Read* (1982), pages 7, 83, and 87.

5 [From page xv]. Refer to the *Dictionary of Simplified American Spelling* (1986), page 9, for documentation confirming that there are 42 sounds in spoken English with over 400 ways to spell these sounds. Refer to the same book, page iv, for the 19 spellings of the *sh* sound. Another book, *The REAL Reason Why Johnny Still Can't Read* (1982), pages 32, 33, and 252, reckons there are 44 sounds in our language with over 600 ways to spell them. Page 96 of the same book has a list of 18 "fairly common" ways to spell the *sh* sound. A third book, *The Mother Tongue* (1990), page 120, is more conservative. It claims there are "some forty sounds in English" with "more than two hundred ways to spell them." That same book and page number reports only 14 spellings for the *sh* sound.

6 [From page 4]. Bede, *A History of the English Church and People*. Translated by Leo Sherley-Price. Revised by R.E. Latham (1968), page 57.

7 [From page 6]. For the makeup of the English Language in its early years and for information that points out that there was very little Celtic influence in early English, refer to the following books: *The Mother Tongue* (1990), page 50; *The Story of English* (1986), page 60; *A Linguistic History of English* (1968), page 54.

8 [From page 6]. Some would say that the Runic-marking system is the earliest form of English writing. Others are a little less positive. The following three points push me into the less-positive camp. a) The Runic system used a different alphabet than we do. b) The Runic system didn't develop into the English-writing system we have today.

c) Runic markings are thought to have been used primarily as magical symbols on weapons and other valuable items. Witch-crafters and devil-worshippers of today use magical symbols on similar items, yet we don't call their markings English writing — even though these markings are sometimes done by English-speaking people in English-speaking countries. For more information on Runic markings, read *The Mother Tongue* (1990), pages 47, 48 and 123; *The Story of the English Language* (1967), page 292; *A History of English Spelling* (1974), pages 1 and 2.

9   [From page 8]. There is some dispute as to who actually brought English writing to England first: Irish monks or St. Augustine. Refer to William Sparkes' book, *Story of the English Language* (1966), page 61, for conformation that the Irish monks arrived in England 40 years after St. Augustine. Also read, *The Mother Tongue* (1990), page 50, and *A History of English Spelling* (1974), pages 3 and 4.

10   [From page 9]. For evidence of Anglo-Saxon legends being injected with Christian themes, refer to, *The English Language* (1985), page 59, by Robert Burchfield.

11   [From page 9]. Some writing has survived in England from before St. Augustine's time. This is Runic writing, not English writing. (See earlier endnote on Runic writing).

12   [From page 12]. D.G. Scragg in his book *A History of English Spelling* (1974), page 6, has this to say about the four dialects: "The spelling systems of the four dialects are sufficiently distinct as to be readily detected, but it

should not be supposed that there appears within each consistency of the order of that pertaining to modern English."

13 [From page 13]. The Old-English Period wasn't totally devoid of silent consonants. See G.H. Vallins' book, *Spelling* (1973), page 42: "h is...inserted where it ought not to have been." For evidence of the rarity of silent consonants in Old English refer to the same book, page 12, and to *The Story of our Language* (1962), page 55, by Henry Alexander.

14 [From page 15]. This nation-wide spelling system emerged from the West Saxon scribal tradition. For more information refer to *The Cambridge History of the English Language* (1992), vol. 2, page 501; *A History of English Spelling* (1974), pages 6 and 7; and *Death by Spelling* (1989), page 14.

15 [From page 15]. Each word in this *Lord's Prayer* passage was not spelled exactly this way every time in late Old English. The passage is simply a typical example of spelling that in late Old English was almost as stable as our own. This particular version of the *Lord's Prayer* was taken from a manuscript dated about the year 1000. The original document (identification # MS Gg 3 28) is located in the Cambridge University Library. For ease of reading, all abbreviations have been expanded and some letters have been changed to their more modern forms. For further clarity, a modern printing font has replaced Old-English handwriting. For a facsimile of the Cambridge manuscript, refer to *A History of English Spelling* (1974), page 6.

16   [From page 16]. King Edgar came to power in 959 and died in 975. For confirmation that he was connected with the stabilization of spelling in late Old English, refer to *The Cambridge History of the English Language* (1992), vol. 1, page 78.

17   [From page 16]. *A History of English Spelling* (1974), page 7. For further information on stable spelling in late Old English read, *The Cambridge History of the English Language* (1992), vol. 1, page 78.

18   [From page 20]. The following books confirm that there was comparatively little English writing during the early Middle-English period: *Spelling* (1973), page 13, and *The Story of English* (1986), pages 74 and 76. The next two books give an account of the extent of the decline of religious, secular, and administrative writing: *A History of English Spelling* (1974), pages 16 and 17, and *A History of the English Language* (1993), pages 118 and 151.

19   [From page 20]. In actuality, the *Anglo-Saxon Chronicle* is one of the publications that did survive for a long while after the invasion. Eventually, however, it too was silenced. Refer to *The Story of English* (1986), page 74, Benet's *Reader's Encyclopedia* (1987), page 36, and *The Oxford English Dictionary* (1989), page xxv.

20   [From page 20]. For additional information on the Robin Hood legends, refer to *Encyclopedia Britannica* (1964), vol. 19, page 358.

21   [From page 26]. Many of the words listed in this chart were Latin words before they became French words. At

the moment of entry into English, some of these words were spelled more than one way in the French language. The French spellings given in this chart are those closest to our Modern-English spellings.

22   [From page 27]. *A History of English Spelling* (1974), page 21. For other information on regional spelling in the middle of the Middle-English period, read *A History of the English Language* (1993), pages 185 and 186.

23   [From page 27]. For information about Orm and his phonetic and consistent spelling, refer to *The New Encyclopedia Britannica* (1993), vol. 8, page 1006, *The Encyclopedia International* (1979) page 190, and *Spelling* (1973), pages 91 and 92. Orm's spelling system has only been found on one manuscript, called the *Ormulum*. The *Ormulum* is a long and dreary poem with 10,000 lines. Many books would place Orm's poem in the early Middle-English period; nevertheless, other books like *The Story of English* (1986), page 76, have the silent period of written English ending about the year 1200 — the same year Orm's manuscript was written.

24   [From page 28]. For information about regional translations in Middle English, refer to *The Story of English* (1986), page 79. Also read, *A History of the English Language* (1993), page 184.

25   [From page 28]. Refer to *The Story of English* (1986), page 79, for corroboration that kyn and ken and kun are Middle-English regional spellings of *kin*. Both *kyn* and *ken* can be found in the writing of Chaucer. Other regionally influenced variants that can be found side by

side in a single region are the vastly different 14th-century spellings of the word *they*: *thai, hi*. For confirmation of this and for information on Middle-English regional spelling in general, refer to the following publications: *A History of the English Language* (1993), page 187; an article written by M.L. Samuels in *English Studies* (1963), vol. 44, page 83; *The Oxford English Dictionary* (1989), under the words *they*, *hi*, and *he*.

[26] [From page 29]. French-influenced spelling customs are English customs that were previously influenced by French customs. Some of these French customs were originally influenced by Latin customs. Many books say that the Latin/French custom of spelling a u-sound with an o was used in English to make certain words easier to read. See *A Linguistic History of English* (1968), page 88, and *Handbook of Middle English* (1964), page 10, by Fernand Mosse. For a differing point of view read, *A History of English Spelling* (1974), page 44.

[27] [From page 30]. *Some* was spelled *sum* before the Normans arrived. Refer to the following books for confirmation: *The Oxford English Dictionary* (1989), vol. 15, page 989, and *A Comprehensive Old English Dictionary* (1982), page 1256.

[28] [From page 30]. *Quick* used to be spelled *cwic* prior to the Norman invasion. Refer to the following dictionaries for proof: *The Oxford English Dictionary* (1989), vol. 13, page 14, and *A Comprehensive Old English Dictionary* (1982), page 270.

[29] [From page 30]. *Dumb* was spelled *dumb* in the Old-English period. This information can be found in the

following books: *English-Old English, Old English-English Dictionary* (1975), page 24, and *The Oxford English Dictionary* (1989), vol. 4, page 1114.

30   [From page 31]. English is generally called a Germanic language; however, as Mario Pei says on page 101 of *The Story of the English Language* (1967), "when it comes to vocabulary, English, thanks to its disguised and naturalized French words, may be said to be half-Romance." For the number of French loan-words that entered English in the Middle-English period, refer to *A Linguistic History of English* (1968), page 265.

31   [From page 31]. Refer to the following publications for information on Chancery spelling and on the growing stability of late Middle-English spelling: *A History of the English Language* (1993), page 190; *An Anthology of Chancery English* (1984), pages xvii, 24–27, 57; *A History of English Spelling* (1974), pages 34, 35, 36, 64, 66; an article written by John H. Fisher in *Speculum* (1977), vol. 52, pages 871 and 896; *The Cambridge History of the English Language* (1992), vol. 2, page 13 and (1999), vol. 3, page 14; and *Death by Spelling* (1989), page 15.

32   [From page 33]. In order to make this transcribed example easier to read, a modern font was used, some letters were changed to more up-to-date forms, and all abbreviations were expanded. For a more complete transcript of this document, refer to *An Anthology of Chancery English* (1984), pages 265 and 266. The original document (identification # SC8/27/1345A) is

held at the Public Records Office in Kew, Richmond, Surrey, England.

³³ [From page 34]. "...gradually becoming phonetic again...", *The Case for Spelling Reform* (1965), page 40.

³⁴ [From page 34]. "We can make the generalization that English spelling in late Middle English was relatively phonetic." *A Linguistic History of English* (1968), page 272.

³⁵ [From page 37]. For various insights and opinions about the early printers' stabilizing or destabilizing affect on spelling, refer to the following books: *The Cambridge History of the English Language* (1999), vol. 3, pages 15, 23 and 24; *Death by Spelling* (1989), page 15; *The English Language* (1985), pages 22 and 176 (footnote 4), by Robert Burchfield; *An Anthology of Chancery English* (1984), pages xvii and 57(footnote 24); Speculum (1977), vol. 52, pages 898 and 899; *A History of English Spelling* (1974), pages 64 to 67; *The Story of the English Language* (1967), pages 50 and 299; *Caxton and His World* (1968), pages 171 thru 175.

³⁶ [From page 38] The N.F. Blake quotation is from *Caxton and His World* (1968), page 174. On the same topic, D.G. Scragg in *A History of English Spelling* (1974), page 64, says: "Rather than further the stabilising movement of the professional scribes, the printers in effect encouraged lack of conformity in spelling." *An Anthology of Chancery English* (1984), refers to the above books on page 57, endnote 24. Also read *The Cambridge History of the English Language* (1999), vol. 3, page 23, and *Death by Spelling* (1989), page 15.

37   [From page 38] For information about Caxton copying the conventions of the manuscripts he was duplicating and translating, read *Caxton and His World* (1968), pages 173 and 174, and *The Oxford Companion to the English Language* (1992), page 201.

38   [From page 38]. For information about Caxton ad-libbing his spelling or using forms from his youth or abroad, see *A History of English Spelling* (1974), pages 66 and 67, *From Old English To Standard English* (1992), page 111, and *The Oxford Companion to the English Language* (1992), page 201.

39   [From page 39]. Caxton in a round-about way did ensure the survival of the spelling of the better scribes because he and the printers who followed him set a precedent by using the same dialect as the better scribes. This would allow future printers to be influenced by the spelling of these better scribes, since they were all writing in the same tongue. For information about 16th-century printers being influenced by the better scribes, see *A History of English Spelling* (1974), page 67, and *The Cambridge Encyclopedia of the English Language* (1995), page 66. For Caxton's choice of the dialect of London as his norm, refer to *The Cambridge Encyclopedia of the English Language* (1995), page 54, and *A History of the English Language* (1993), page 190. For information about Caxton's lack of standardization, refer to *The Cambridge Encyclopedia of the English Language* (1995), page 57, *The Oxford Companion to the English Language* (1992), page 200, *From Old English to Standard English* (1992), page 111, and *Caxton and His World* (1968), page 173, footnote 2.

40   [From page 39]. *A Linguistic History of English* (1968), page 272.

41   [From page 39]. *A History of English Spelling* (1974), page 66.

42   [From page 40]. This transcribed example only shows the inconsistencies on one page. There are inconsistencies on most of Caxton's pages, if not every one. Furthermore, the inconsistencies increase exponentially when pages and books are compared. This page is only a typical example of Caxton's work. Sometimes he had more and sometimes he had fewer inconsistencies per page. In order to make this example easier to read, all abbreviations were expanded and some letters were changed to more up-to-date forms. A more modern font was also used. For a facsimile of this page in its original form, refer to *Caxton: England's First Publisher* (1976), page 62, by N.F. Blake. The example given is the second page of the prologue to the book *Eneydos*. William Caxton translated *Eneydos* from French into English in 1490. It was printed the same year.

43   [From page 41]. I have called this third destabilization period "relatively minor" because (as mentioned in earlier text) even the better scribes already had abundant inconsistency before Caxton came along. Also, compared to the other two destabilizing periods, this one was by far the lesser of the three.

44   [From page 41]. These variations came from *Le Morte de'Arthur*, printed by Caxton in 1485. A microfilm of this edition (catalog #: PML 17560 ChL No. f.1782) can be

obtained from Pierpont Morgan Library in New York City.

45 [From page 42]. Some of the printers and typesetters of the late 15th century were more stable than Caxton and his typesetters. These more stable individuals, however, added little to our stability because they were still very inconsistent. Furthermore, what stability they had was often different from each other and from the better scribes. For additional information on early printers and typesetters, refer to the following books: *The Cambridge Encyclopedia of the English Language* (1995), page 66; *A History of English Spelling* (1974), pages 64–67; *The Biography and Typography of William Caxton* (1971), page 66; *English books and readers*, 1475–1557 (1952), pages 181 and 182.

46 [From page 44]. Caxton must have known about the more stable spelling of the better scribes because he encountered their spelling every time he duplicated their manuscripts. He also worked close to the Royal Chancery — the original source of this stabilization. It is obvious from this that Caxton simply wasn't interested in spelling. For Caxton's lack of interest in spelling and his connections with professional scribes, see *Caxton and his World* (1968), pages 171, 173, and 175.

47 [From page 46]. Refer to the following publications for varying opinions on the topic of Caxton and the early printers being more stable or less stable than the scribes: *The Encyclopedia Britannica* (1964), vol. 8, page 543; *Caxton and His World* (1968), page 174; *Spelling* (1973), pages 13 and 64; *A History of English Spelling* (1974),

pages 64 and 66; *The English Language* (1985), pages 22 and 176 footnote 4, by Robert Burchfield; *The English Language* (1988), page 75, by David Crystal; *Death by Spelling* (1989), page 15; *The Cambridge History of the English Language* (1999), vol. 3, pages 15, 23, 24, and 25.

48   [From page 50]. This paragraph, taken from *The English Secretorie* (1586), has been retyped using more modern letters to make it easier to read. For a facsimile of this paragraph, refer to page 14 of *The English Secretorie* (1967), by The Scolar Press Ltd.

49   [From page 51]. For an example of some of the confusion caused by line justification, refer to the book *Spelling*, page 58.

50   [From page 53]. For information about foreign words entering English during the Renaissance, refer to the following books: *A History of the English Language* (1993), page 222; *The Story of English* (1986), page 95; *The REAL Reason Why Johnny Still Can't Read* (1982), page 79.

51   [From page 55]. In this chart, "English words" means home-grown or loan-words that were part of the English language before being influenced by Latin spelling during the Renaissance. "Latin spelling" means spelling that came to us from the Latin language. Many Latin words were originally borrowed from the Greek language. The correct spelling of anchor in Latin is *ancora*. Unfortunately, it was often incorrectly spelled *anchora* and our English spelling was taken from that. As with many early Modern-English Latinized words, it has not

been absolutely proven that the 16th-century spelling, *subtle*, came directly from Latin, or whether it came through the French language first. Either way, it was still influenced by the Latin word *subtilis*.

52   [From page 56]. *A History of English Spelling* (1974), page 52.

53   [From page 57]. David Mellinkoff, *The Language of the Law* (1963), page 190.

54   [From page 59]. Some false-etymology spellings are also called analogy spellings. For information on both refer to *Spelling* (1973), pages 23 and 24.

55   [From page 59]. *The Oxford Companion to the English Language* (1992), page 453, has the Great Vowel Shift ending about 1600. Other publications agree approximately with this date. Others have it ending earlier than 1550 or as late as 1750. Some say it slowly continues even to this day. See *Microsoft Encarta* (1995), *A History of the English Language* (1993), page 234, and *The REAL Reason Why Johnny Still Can't Read* (1982), page 75.

56   [From page 61]. Some of these strange vowel spellings were not fully developed by the end of the 16th century; nevertheless, their strangeness is assumed to be caused by the vowel shifting that went on before then. For an in-depth description of the spelling anomalies created or encouraged during the time of the Great Vowel Shift, refer to the following books: *Early Modern English* (1976), pages 292–306, by Charles Barber; *A Linguistic*

History of English (1968), pages 99–106; *The REAL Reason Why Johnny Still Can't Read* (1982), page 78; *The Mother Tongue* (1990), pages 92–94; *A History of the English Language* (1993), page 234. For excellent charts documenting the changes caused by the Great Vowel Shift, refer to *A History of English* (1970), page 174, by Barbara M. H. Strang and *The English Language* (1949), page 92, by C. L. Wrenn. Both these charts are recommended by Robert Burchfield in *The English Language* (1985), pages 23 and 176, as convenient tabulations of the main changes brought about by the Great Vowel Shift.

57   [From page 65]. This page is from William Shakespeare's *Lucrece* (1594). A facsimile of this page can be found in *Shakespeare's Poems* (1964), page 148, by Yale University. The printer of this 1594 poem was Richard Field. Mr. Field was one of the more careful and consistent London printers of the late 16th century. Here are a few of the many other inconsistent spellings in Mr. Field's 1594 publication. The numbers in parenthesis correspond to the page numbers where these spellings can be found in the facsimile book, *Shakespeare's Poems* (1964): *roman* (63), *romane* (77), *romaine* (87); *romains* (149), *romaines* (151); *floud* (143), *flood* (146); *wold* (65), *would* (65); *aunswer* (67), *answer* (139); *straunger* (68), *stranger* (140); *ech* (77), *each* (78). Here are the "different spellings" (and facsimile book page numbers) that correspond to the words in bold type in my example: *deep* (126), *dum* (85), *vppon* (71), *tong* (145), *controull* (87), *keep* (81), *doe* (70), *poore* (147), *aide* (144), *hee* (87), *sayd* (151), *back* (142), *weepe* (128), *laie* (75), *she* (143), *awaie* (75), *saie* (144).

58   [From page 68]. Refer to *The English Language in America* (1960), pages 328, 329, and 348 for general information on early American spelling.

59   [From page 70]. To make this transcribed cover page easier to read, a modern font was used and some letters were changed to a more up-to-date form. The almanac to which this cover page belongs is associated with at least three firsts: it was printed by America's first printer, it contains the name of America's first bookseller, and it is the first American book to contain the name of its printer. A facsimile of the original cover page can be found in the book *Printing in America* (1965). Matthew Day's surname was sometimes spelled *Daye*.

60   [From page 71]. For information regarding 17th-century stabilization, refer to the following books: *A History of English Spelling* (1974), page 80; *A History of the English Language* (1993), page 208. For information about American spelling never differing much from British spelling, refer to *The American Language* (1962), page 380, and *The English Language in America* (1960), pages 328, 329, and 348.

61   [From page 72]. To make this transcribed example easier to read, a modern font was used and some letters were changed to a more up-to-date form. The spelling in this example is exactly as the first edition of *Gulliver's Travels* (1726) by Jonathan Swift. For a facsimile of this page (in its 1726 format), refer to the second-last page of *Gulliver's Travels* (1976), edited by Colin McKelvie.

62   [From page 73]. For Edmund Coote's importance to the
stabilization of English spelling, refer to the following
books: *The Oxford Companion to the English Language*
(1992), page 974, and *A History of English Spelling*
(1974), pages 62, 63, and 75–78. For other information
about Edmund Coote and his spelling book, along with
information on the first (non-comprehensive) spelling
book — *Abc for Chyldren* (1551–58) — refer to *A
Linguistic History of English* (1968), pages 273 and 283.

63   [From page 73]. In the 1596 edition of Coote's book there
are still some minor differences in spelling from that of
the present day — for example, doubling of final
consonants, addition of final e, use of ie for y. However,
more than half of his words are spelled exactly as now.
The spelling in subsequent editions of this book became
more and more modern as the 17th century progressed.

64   [From page 73]. Information about Edmund Coote
selecting spelling from the variants most frequently in
print can be found in D.G. Scragg's book, *A History of
English Spelling* (1974), pages 77 and 78. For a broader
look at what Edmund Coote did, refer to Robert A.
Peters' book *A Linguistic History of English* (1968), page
273 and 283; and the preface to *The English Schoole-
Maister* (1596), by Edmund Coote.

65   [From page 78]. Refer to the following publications for
information regarding Edmund Coote's influence on *A
Table Alphabeticall* (1604): *The Encyclopedia Britanica*
(1998), vol.18, page 278; *The English Language* (1985),
page 82, by Robert Burchfield, the opening note from *The
English Schoole-Maister* (1968), a facsimile of Edmund
Coote's spelling book by Scolar Press.

66   [From page 80]. The similar inquiry was quoted in the book *Spelling* (1973), page 120.

67   [From page 81]. Private spelling in personal letters lagged behind professional spelling in published books and government documents, etc.; nevertheless, by the end of the 17th century many everyday people were already affected by irrational stabilization. For information about children learning spelling at school in the 17th century refer to, *The Cambridge Encyclopedia of the English Language* (1995), page 67.

68   [From page 87]. Samuel Johnson, *A Dictionary of the English Language* (1755), preface page 1.

69   [From page 88]. Samuel Johnson, *A Dictionary of the English Language* (1755), preface page 2.

70   [From page 89]. Quoted in *The Little, Brown Book of Anecdotes* (1985), page 312.

71   [From page 89]. Quoted by Bill Bryson in *The Mother Tongue* (1990), page 172.

72   [From page 90]. Samuel Johnson, *A Dictionary of the English Language* (1755), preface page 10.

73   [From page 92]. H.L. Mencken, *The American Language* (1962), page 380.

74   [From page 92]. For information pertaining to Americans following British spelling conventions in the 18th

century, refer to *The American Language* (1962), page 380, and *The Discoverers* (1983), page 555.

75   [From page 93]. For further reading on American spelling tendencies in the 18th and early 19th centuries, refer to *The Mother Tongue* (1990), pages 155 and 156, and *A History of the English Language* (1993), page 364.

76   [From page 93]. For more detailed information on the spelling used in the *Declaration of Independence*, refer to *The Politics of American English*, 1776 - 1850 (1986), page 21.

77   [From page 94]. The document portrayed is a transcript of the first three sentences of the first printing of *The Declaration of Independence*. John Dunlap did the printing on July 5, 1776, the day after the final handwritten draft was completed by the United States congress. My transcript uses a modern font to make the document easier to read, however, the spelling and capitalization are exactly as the original printing. A facsimile of this historic 1776 printing can be found at the beginning of *A Casebook on The Declaration of Independence* (1967), by Robert Ginsberg.

78   [From page 95]. For further comments on the development of the American accent, refer to *A History of the English Language* (1993), page 358 and The Mother Tongue (1990), page 166.

79   [From page 95]. For debate on the extent to which other languages were considered as the official language in America, refer to *The Story of English* (1986), page 239;

The Mother Tongue (1990), page 167; and *The Cambridge Encyclopedia of Language* (1987), page 365.

80 [From page 97]. Refer to the following books for further information on the first dictionaries printed in America: *The English Language in America* (1960), pages 353, 356, and 357; *A Linguistic History of English* (1968), page 289; *The Politics of American English, 1776–1850* (1986), page 49.

81 [From page 100]. *The Encyclopedia America* (1990), vol. 28, page 561.

82 [From page 101]. *Spelling* (1973), page 184. Other books that discuss the superficial differences between American and British spelling are *The English Language in America* (1960), pages 328, 329, and 348; *A History of the English Language* (1963), page 428; and *The REAL Reason Why Johnny Still Can't Read* (1982), pages 86 and 87.

83 [From page 102]. I'm talking here about simplified spelling organizations whose purpose is to simplify the spelling of the *English* language. Many other languages like Russian, Turkish, and Dutch have already had their spelling simplified. So the organizations that brought about the changes in those languages were certainly more successful, if not more determined, than any English spelling organization. For information about spelling that has been simplified in other languages, see *The REAL Reason Why Johnny Still Can't Read* (1982), page 87, and *Watching English Change* (1994), pages 136,139, and 140. The main organization in the United States that

has goals to simplify English spelling is the American Literacy Council, based in New York City. American Literacy Council is the current name for a string of simplified spelling organizations that date back to 1876. These organizations in reverse chronological order are: The American Language Academy (1984), Phonemic Spelling Council (1971), Simplified Spelling Association (1946), Simplified Spelling Board (1906), and Spelling Reform Association (1876). The British simplified spelling organization is called The Simplified Spelling Society. It was founded in 1908 and is based in London.

84   [From page 106]. Franklin's influence on Webster can be read about in the following books: *A History of the English Language* (1993), pages 363 and 364; *The Story of English* (1986), page 237.

85   [From page 106]. In calling Webster "the father of American spelling" I have taken into account that he is generally considered to have played the starring roll in differentiating between American and British spelling. See *Spelling* (1973), pages 186 thru 190, *A History of the English Language* (1993), page 363, and *The Story of English* (1986), page 242. H.L. Mencken in *The American Language* (1962), page 399, calls him the "father of the simplified spelling movement."

86   [From page 108]. To be truly factual, in the 20th century we have more than two English spelling customs. Nevertheless, as far as global influence is concerned, the British and American systems are in a league of their own. Refer to the following books for information about the dominance of British and American spelling, other systems that are in use in other countries, and which

146

countries use which system: *Watching English Change* (1994), pages 134 and 135; *The Story of English* (1986), pages 38, 245, and 317; *The English Language and Images of Matter* (1972), pages 51 and 52.

87   [From page 108]. There is some American influence on British spelling. American sources are said by some to exaggerate this influence while British sources are said to play it down. Refer to the following books for additional insight: *Watching English Change* (1994), pages 134, 135, and 136; *A Guide To The Oxford English Dictionary* (1993), page 175; *The Mother Tongue* (1990), page 175; *The English Language* (1988), page 247.

88   [From page 109]. When *The Oxford English Dictionary* first came out it was called *A New English Dictionary on Historical Principles*. In 1933 it was renamed *The Oxford English Dictionary*.

89   [From page 109]. *A New English Dictionary on Historical Principles* (now known as *The Oxford English Dictionary*), vol. 1, page xxix, had this to say about its choice of spelling: "Every Main Word is treated, once for all, under its modern current or most usual spelling." Notwithstanding this statement, there are a few instances in that publication where spellings were chosen for their pronunciation or etymology rather than for their conformity to the current or most usual standard. These instances, however, are rare. There are also some main word spellings that appear to be American-influenced. Some of these spellings can be traced to older British or ancient Greek spellings, or to some other non-American source. For further insight into these things refer to the

following books: *A Guide to The Oxford English Dictionary* (1993), page 175; *Spelling* (1973), pages 150-183; *The Mother Tongue* (1990), page 160.

90   [From page 109]. When I say British spelling is paralyzed, I mean the basic core of British spelling is paralyzed. Some spellings have changed slightly since 1928. Also a few spellings in the 1928 *Oxford English Dictionary* have always been ignored by the majority of Britons. Refer to the following books for additional information: *The Oxford English Dictionary* (1989), page xiv, and *The Mother Tongue* (1990), page 160.

91   [From page 111]. For confirmation that the 1928 *Oxford English Dictionary* chose "jail" and "program" and a few other spellings against the accepted norm, refer to *A Guide to The Oxford English Dictionary* (1993), Page 175. I use the phrase "suspiciously American" because *The Oxford English Dictionary* and *A Guide to The Oxford English Dictionary* never say outright that the preferred spellings that look American in *The Oxford English Dictionary* are actually American or American-influenced. I also say "suspiciously American" because *The Oxford English Dictionary*'s preference for words with -*ize* endings (realize, civilize, authorize, etc.), rather than -*ise* endings (realise, civilise, authorise etc.), could be due to Johnson spelling most of these types of words the -*ize* way in his 1755 dictionary. Or it could be due to Britain long having a conflict between these two types of spellings. Then again it could be due to Webster's influence, or a mixture of all three. American spelling can definitely be seen in *The Oxford English Dictionary*'s second choice of spelling, especially in words ending in -*our*. For further insight, refer to *A New English*

Dictionary on Historical Principles (1884–1928), under the words *colour* and *favour*.

92   [From page 111]. The 1928 *Oxford English Dictionary* had some preferred spellings that deviated from the acceptable spelling of the day. Many of these spellings have been ignored or are not widely accepted by the British public. This doesn't mean British reform is pointless. It means the British should follow the American example: change the spelling in the dictionaries and at the same time change the spelling in the school spelling books. For information about dictionaries having their spelling ignored refer to *The Mother Tongue* (1990), page 160.

93   [From page 112]. Murray wasn't unaware of the irony that a Scotsman was responsible for downgrading Johnson's dictionary from its number one position in Britain — he often joked about it himself. Refer to his granddaughter's book, *Caught in the Web of Words* (1977), page 188, for an example of this.

94   [From page 115]. A version of this statement can be found in *The Mother Tongue* (1990), page 174. It reads: "American English... is nonetheless a foreign tongue and should be treated as such." That statement is a paraphrase of what H.W. and F.G. Fowler said in *The King's English* (1931). Page 33 of the 1962 edition of this book put it this way: "Americanisms are foreign words, and should be so treated." For other more up-to-date passages that highlight British dislike of American English, refer to the following books: *The Mother Tongue* (1990), pages 174 and 175, and *The Story of English* (1986), page 343.

ABOUT THE AUTHOR

Niall McLeod Waldman was born and educated in Glasgow, Scotland. In 1974, he immigrated with his family to North America. He is married with three grown children and one grandchild. As a long-time parent and homework-helper, he has struggled to answer his and other children's questions about why spelling is so complex. This book is his response to these never-ending inquiries.

Spelling Dearest is the author's first book. His lengthy association with literacy and simplified-spelling organizations, coupled with ten years of research, prepared him well for this subject. Niall is an active member of ALC (American Literacy Council) and SSS (Simplified Spelling Society).

The skillfully illustrated pen and ink sketches found throughout this book were created by the author. His artwork has been featured in many publications, and appears in public and private collections around the world.

To contact the author with comments or questions:

Email:	nmwaldman@spellingdearest.com
	or nmwaldman@aol.com
Smail:	Niall McLeod Waldman
	2059 Pratt's Marina Road
	RR3 Lakefield, K0L 2H0
	Ontario, Canada
Phone:	(705) 652 7943
Net:	www.spellingdearest.com

Printed in the United States
44909LVS00005BA/142-144